SCHOLASTIC
LITERACY SKILLS

Vocabulary
Year 4

TERMS AND CONDITIONS

IMPORTANT – PERMITTED USE AND WARNINGS – READ CAREFULLY BEFORE USING

Minimum system requirements:

- PC or Mac with CD-ROM drive (16x speed recommended) and 512MB RAM
- P4 or G4 processor
- Windows 2000/XP/Vista or Mac OSX 10.3 or later

For all technical support queries, please phone Scholastic Customer Services on 0845 6039091.

Author
Pam Dowson

Development editor
Rachel Mackinnon

Copy editor
Sarah Sodhi

Assistant editors
Louise Titley and Suzanne Adams

CD-ROM design and development team
Joy Monkhouse, Anna Oliwa,
Micky Pledge, Rebecca Male,
Allison Parry, James Courier,
Jim Peacock/Beehive Illustration

Series designers
Shelley Best and Anna Oliwa

Book layout
Sonja Bagley and Shelley Best

Illustrations
Catherine Ward

Designed using Adobe Indesign
Published by Scholastic Ltd, Book End,
Range Road, Witney,
Oxfordshire OX29 0YD
www.scholastic.co.uk

Printed by Bell & Bain Ltd, Glasgow
Text © 2010 Pam Dowson
© 2010 Scholastic Ltd
1 2 3 4 5 6 7 8 9 0 0 1 2 3 4 5 6 7 8 9

British Library Cataloguing-in-Publication Data
A catalogue record for this book is available from
the British Library.
ISBN 978-1407-10225-2

Mixed Sources
Product group from well-managed
forests and other controlled sources
www.fsc.org Cert no. TT-COC-002769
© 1996 Forest Stewardship Council

Every effort has been made to trace copyright holders for the
works reproduced in this book, and the publishers apologise for
any inadvertent omissions.

Extracts from Primary National Strategy's Primary Framework for
Literacy (2006) http://nationalstrategies.standards.dcsf.gov.uk/
primary/primaryframework/ © Crown copyright. Reproduced under
the terms of the Click Use Licence.

Due to the nature of the web, we cannot guarantee the content or
links of any site mentioned. We strongly recommend that teachers
check websites before using them in the classroom.

Contents

Chapter 1
Synonyms and antonyms

Chapter 2
Word origins

Chapter 3
Grammar

Chapter 4
Cross-curricular vocabulary

Chapter 5
Fun with words

Introduction

Scholastic Literacy Skills: Vocabulary series

According to David Crystal, a major contributor to our understanding of how language works, by the age of five most children have an active vocabulary of over 4,000 words. He suggests that children learn, on average, three or four new words a day, and that 'A child reading Roald Dahl stories at age nine is being exposed to over 10,000 different words' (*How Language Works*, 2005). It is obviously important that children continue to add to their personal lexicon in order to both understand and make themselves understood, in many contexts. But as Crystal also tells us, definitions for these new words are not learned straight away; rather children need time and opportunities for new words to be added to their vocabulary, which is where we, as teachers, have a vital role to play. The words and activities in this book have been specifically designed to support that role.

Teaching vocabulary

By Year 4, we expect most children to have some understanding of how words are classified – as nouns, verbs, adjectives, adverbs and connectives, for example. This enables us to use this 'metalanguage' when we talk about words, particularly in relation to their own writing, and to developing vocabulary. Because of this, and because we are conscious that children need to know these technical terms, there is a danger that we might compartmentalise words into these divisions when we are teaching, but when children learn new words, they need a context within which to understand them. For example when they first come across the adjective *enthusiastic*, it becomes part of the set of words within their experience that have a similar meaning, such as *keen* or *eager*, usually associated with narrative or poetry. In this way vocabulary is extended, providing greater choices for both speaking and writing as well as aiding understanding when reading.

For that reason, the activities in this book have been linked to a wide range of text types found in the Primary National Strategy for Literacy for Year 4. The activities can therefore be used in conjunction with the Units in the Framework for Literacy, or to support other curriculum areas.

About the product

This book contains five chapters of activities for teaching vocabulary. Each chapter focuses on a different vocabulary area, and is organised into four sections with clear objectives, background information for the concepts taught, teaching ideas, and photocopiable pages for use in whole-class teaching, with groups or for independent work. Each chapter also has a poster, assessment, Word of the week section and Fun with words sections. The word bank at the end of the book provides banks of words to be used in games and other activities linked to this book.

Posters

Each chapter has one poster. These posters are related to the subject of the chapter and should be displayed and used for reference throughout the work on the chapter. The poster notes (on the chapter introduction page) offer suggestions for how they could be used. There are black and white versions in the book and full-colour versions on the CD-ROM for you to print out or display on your whiteboard.

Assessment

Each chapter has an assessment section. It summarises the objectives and activities in the section, provides pointers on observation and record keeping and includes one assessment photocopiable page (which is also printable from the CD-ROM with answers, where appropriate).

Word of the week and Fun with words

For each chapter there are notes on Word of the week and Fun with words. Word of the week provides one word you might like to focus on related to each section. Fun with words provides general activities to use with your class throughout work on the chapter.

Word bank

The word bank at the end of each book provides a list of words you might like to use in games or other activities.

Activities

Each section contains three activities. These activities all take the form of a photocopiable page which is in the book.

Each photocopiable page is also included on the CD-ROM for you to display or print out (these pages are also provided with answers where appropriate). Many of the photocopiable pages have linked interactive activities on the CD-ROM. These interactive activities are designed to act as starter activities to the lesson, giving whole-class support on the information being taught. However, they can work equally well as plenary activities, reviewing the work the children have just completed.

Differentiation

Activities in this book are not differentiated explicitly, although teacher notes may make suggestions for support or extension. Many of the activities can be used with the whole class with extra support provided through differentiated and open-ended questions, use of additional adults, mixed-ability paired or group work or additional input and consolidation before and/or after lessons. Some children may need support with the reading aspects of tasks in order to participate in the vocabulary objectives.

Using the CD-ROM

Below are brief guidance notes for using the CD-ROM. For more detailed information, see **How to use** on the start-up screen, or **Help** on the relevant screen for information about that page.

The CD-ROM follows the structure of the book and contains:

- All of the photocopiable pages.
- All of the poster pages in full colour.
- Photocopiable pages (with answers where appropriate).
- Thirty interactive on-screen activities linked to the photocopiable pages.

Getting started

To begin using the CD-ROM, simply place it in your CD- or DVD-ROM drive. Although the CD-ROM should auto-run, if it fails to do so, navigate to the drive and double-click on the red **Start** icon.

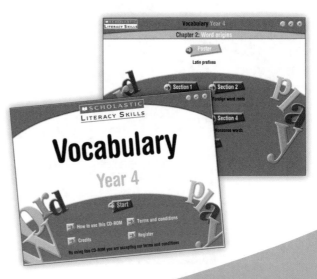

Start-up screen

The start-up screen is the first screen that appears. Here you can access: terms and conditions, registration links, how to use the CD-ROM and credits. If you agree to the terms and conditions, click **Start** to continue.

Main menu

The main menu provides links to all of the chapters or all of the resources. Clicking on the relevant **Chapter** icon will take you to the chapter screen where you can access the posters and the chapter's sections. Clicking on **All resources** will take you to a list of all the resources, where you can search by key word or chapter for a specific resource.

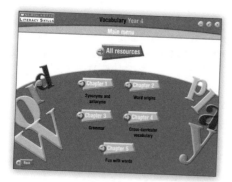

Section screen

Upon choosing a section from the chapter screen, you are taken to a list of resources for that section. Here you can access all of the photocopiable pages related to that section as well as the linked interactive activities.

Resource finder

The **Resource finder** lists all of the resources on the CD-ROM. You can:

- Select a chapter and/or section by selecting the appropriate title from the drop-down menus.
- Search for key words by typing them into the search box.
- Scroll up or down the list of resources to locate the required resource.
- To launch a resource, simply click once on its row on the screen.

Navigation

The resources (poster pages, photocopiable pages and interactive activities) all open in separate windows on top of the menu screen. This means that you can have more than one resource open at the same time. To close a resource, click on the **x** in the top right-hand corner of the screen. To return to the menu screen you can either close or minimise a resource.

Closing a resource will not close the program. However, if you are in a menu screen, then clicking on the **x** will close the program. To return to a previous menu screen, you need to click on the **Back** button.

Whiteboard tools

The CD-ROM comes with its own set of whiteboard tools for use on any whiteboard. These include:

- Pen tool
- Highlighter tool
- Eraser
- Sticky note

Click on the **Tools** button at the foot of the screen to access these tools.

Printing

Print the resources by clicking on the Print button. The photocopiable pages print as full A4 portrait pages, but please note if you have a landscape photocopiable page or poster you need to set the orientation to landscape in your print preferences. The interactive activities will print what is on the screen. For a full A4 printout you need to set the orientation to landscape in your print preferences.

Framework objectives

Chapter	Page	Section	Literacy skills objective	Strand 1: Tell stories effectively and convey detailed information coherently for listeners.	Strand 2: Identify how talk varies with age, familiarity, gender and purpose.	Strand 7: Use knowledge of word structures and origins to develop their understanding of word meanings.	Strand 7: Explain how writers use figurative and expressive language to create images and atmosphere.	Strand 9: Show imagination through the language used to create emphasis, humour, atmosphere or suspense.	Strand 9: Choose and combine words, images and other features for particular effects.	Strand 10: Use adverbs and conjunctions to establish cohesion within paragraphs.
Chapter 1	12	The impact of synonyms on audience	To understand the term *synonym*. To use synonyms in writing.	✓	✓			✓	✓	
	16	Retelling a story in your own words	To tell stories effectively and convey detailed information coherently for listeners. To show imagination through the language used to create emphasis, humour, atmosphere or suspense.	✓	✓			✓		
	20	Avoiding nice and said	To explain how writers use expressive language to create atmosphere. To learn how to use a thesaurus effectively.	✓	✓		✓	✓		
	24	Words related to everyday life	To identify how talk varies with purpose. To show imagination through the language used to create emphasis, humour, atmosphere or suspense.	✓	✓		✓	✓		
Chapter 2	35	Interesting and unusual prefixes	To use a knowledge of prefixes to develop understanding of word meanings.			✓				
	39	Foreign word roots	To use a knowledge of word origins to develop an understanding of word meanings. To be aware of the influence of other languages on English.			✓			✓	
	43	Old and new words	To realise that vocabulary changes over time and to discuss why this happens.			✓				
	47	Nonsense words	To use knowledge of word meanings and origins to write meanings for invented words. To use knowledge of prefixes and word roots to invent new words in context. To demonstrate an understanding of word derivations.			✓	✓			

Framework objectives

Page	Section	Literacy skills objective	Strand 1: Tell stories effectively and convey detailed information coherently for listeners.	Strand 2: Identify how talk varies with age, familiarity, gender and purpose.	Strand 7: Use knowledge of word structures and origins to develop their understanding of word meanings.	Strand 7: Explain how writers use figurative and expressive language to create images and atmosphere.	Strand 9: Show imagination through the language used to create emphasis, humour, atmosphere or suspense.	Strand 9: Choose and combine words, images and other features for particular effects.	Strand 10: Use adverbs and conjunctions to establish cohesion within paragraphs.
58	Alternative verbs	To use alternative words that are more accurate and interesting than the most common choices. To identify and use more powerful and interesting verbs.							
62	Adjectives and adverbs	To identify adverbs, use them in writing and understand the impact of them. To use adjectives to improve written descriptions.			✓	✓	✓		✓
66	Formal and informal words	To decide how to choose the best words for different audiences. To understand the difference between writing for formal and informal purposes.				✓	✓		
70	Connectives	To use connectives to create compound sentences.				✓	✓		✓
81	Geography	To use vocabulary relating to settlement, the environment and mapping.			✓				
85	History	To use vocabulary relating to the passage of time, aspects of society, and fact and opinion.			✓				
89	Mathematics	To use vocabulary relating to the four operations, shape and handling data.			✓				
93	Science	To use vocabulary relating to the explanation of scientific processes.			✓				
104	Signs and symbols	To combine words and images to communicate meaning.			✓	✓	✓	✓	
108	Portmanteau words	To use word knowledge to create new words.			✓	✓	✓	✓	
112	Real words and nonsense words	To investigate unusual uses of written language.			✓	✓	✓	✓	
116	Word fun	To make contextual use of language knowledge.			✓	✓	✓	✓	

Chapter 3 — pages 58, 62, 66, 70
Chapter 4 — pages 81, 85, 89, 93
Chapter 5 — pages 104, 108, 112, 116

Using vocabulary

Using and developing children's vocabulary

Use these notes to support the teaching of vocabulary in this book.

EAL note

Having bilingual dictionaries and thesauruses will prove particularly helpful for EAL learners at this stage. If they are getting to grips with the basis of a second language, extending beyond basic vocabulary is likely to prove particularly difficult, but they can still be encouraged to do this in their home language, which can help develop deeper understanding of the second language

Encourage children learning EAL to share their home languages with native English speakers, particularly in the area of word origins, to show how languages often borrow from each other. EAL speakers, and their parents, could help to compile illustrated class dictionaries using the new vocabulary, where appropriate.

Specific words

Before using the photocopiable sheets, see how they link with content-based units that you may be planning so that you can work on some of the new vocabulary in advance, for example, in history or geography. This is particularly useful for words that can be used cross-curricularly.

Each chapter has a Word of the week section, where vocabulary matched to the age group is introduced. The chosen words can be used in a variety of contexts, with suggestions being given for reinforcing children's working knowledge of each word. These words could form a regular part of the week's learning, with perhaps one word being introduced every other week, so that there is opportunity to embed it, across a range of contexts, before learning the next word.

Word learning strategies

Some of the activities assume that children know how to use dictionaries and thesauruses. Ensure there are a range of these available, particularly with differentiation in mind. A useful addition to the classroom when working on word origins and prefixes, would be a children's version of a dictionary of word origins. In addition, roots, prefixes and suffixes could be used as the basis for spellings to be learned. As new words are introduced, look for opportunities to use them yourself, in a range of contexts where appropriate, in order to reinforce pronunciation and definitions

Concentrate on teaching three types of words

Decide, in relation to your own class, into which of the categories 'important', 'useful', or 'difficult' the words fall in each chapter or section. 'Important' words would be those that are the most important to understanding concepts being taught which all children should learn. 'Useful' words would be those which children might use but they would not be classed as vital to understanding. 'Difficult' words might be homophones, idiomatic or words with particularly difficult spelling patterns or pronunciation. You should focus most on the words you consider to be important for the whole class, groups or individuals to learn.

Word consciousness

Many of the activities and further ideas in the book are designed to create a curiosity about words and an enjoyment in learning more about them in a wide variety of ways. Look for opportunities where these ideas can be used in order to reinforce the new vocabulary both in planned sessions and informally.

Chapter 1

Synonyms and antonyms

Introduction

This chapter focuses on commonly used words, of which children have a working knowledge, and develops this to extend their vocabulary. Focusing on synonyms (and some antonyms) gives children the confidence to use more unusual and interesting words than those on which they often rely. Children are encouraged to use their senses, consider the audience by writing in a variety of roles, and make use of a thesaurus. There are opportunities for paired work and drama activities as well as a wide range of writing experiences.

Poster notes

Synonyms for said (page 11)

The poster provides a range of different words to be used in place of *said*. There are three levels: a core collection that can be used to support less confident speakers and writers, a middle collection and a more adventurous set of alternatives that can challenge much more confident learners. As well as offering support for writing, the poster can be used to support speaking and listening activities, such as saying sentences in the manner of the word and letting others guess which word is being demonstrated.

In this chapter

Synonyms and antonyms

Synonyms for said

Can you move through the levels to increase your synonym rating?

Level 3

hesitated   blurted out   ordered
stated   claimed   began   continued   questioned
persisted   ventured   queried   hinted
protested   complained

Level 2

muttered   snarled   cackled
moaned   boasted   croaked   grumbled
mumbled   demanded   nagged
bellowed   laughed   suggested

Level 1

called   shouted   answered
cried   asked
yelled   wondered
whispered

Illustrations © 2010, Catherine Ward.

The impact of synonyms on audience

Objective

To understand the term *synonym*. To use synonyms in writing.

Background knowledge

Synonyms are words that have the same or similar meanings, so that one word can be substituted by another word that is synonymous to it, such as using *huge* or *enormous* in place of *big*. However, be aware that they can sometimes convey slightly different meanings, for example, *hobbled* is a synonym for *walked* but does not have the same meaning as *sauntered*. You can make good use of the fact that the words *synonym*, *similar* and *same* all begin with the letter 's' to help children understand and remember them. Having a range of thesauruses in your classroom is extremely helpful for developing knowledge of synonyms.

Activities

In this section the children begin to widen their vocabulary by using alternatives to common words and considering how word choice impacts upon the reader. The activities provide opportunities to use a thesaurus.

● **Photocopiable page 13 'Holiday postcard'**
This postcard activity provides a good introduction to the need for synonyms and includes a list of synonyms to offer as a scaffold. Let the children work in pairs to identify the words that could be changed, before working individually on their redraft. Then ask them to read their rewritten postcard to compare word choices.

● **Photocopiable page 14 'Tricky twins'**
The children may be unfamiliar with the language used in school reports, so read some made-up examples before they do the activity. To help the children think of synonyms, a thesaurus would be useful, but try to provide several different versions to allow for differentiation as well as providing a wider search facility. Encourage the children to use generally positive language.

● **Photocopiable page 15 'Taking a walk'**
This activity provides another good opportunity to use a thesaurus. Discuss how a word can have more than one synonym. Before commencing this activity, read some examples of descriptive poetry. Discuss how using the senses adds to the detail that is possible in the poem.

Further ideas

● **Postcard display:** Create a display by asking the children to bring in postcards. Can they find any examples of synonyms or examples of the word *nice* being used?
● **Celebrity reports:** Invite the children to write reports on celebrities of their choice. Encourage them to use synonyms to avoid repetition.

What's on the CD-ROM

On the CD-ROM you will find:
● Printable versions of all three photocopiable pages.
● Interactive versions of 'Holiday postcard' and 'Taking a walk'.

The impact of synonyms on audience

Holiday postcard

■ Read this postcard. Highlight the words you could change to improve it.

Dear Ali,

This is a nice place. The hotel is good and the food
is nice. There is very good ice cream! My room
is quite big and the bed is nice. Our journey was
okay but a bit long, though the views from the
plane were good. The weather is hot. The swimming
pool is big and the water is warm there. The
beach is good, but the sea is quite cold. There's
a sandcastle competition tomorrow that should
be fun. Yesterday we went to an old castle that I
thought would be fun but it was not very good. The
only bad thing is we are only here for a week.

See you soon,

Sam

_____

_____

_____

_____

_____

_____

■ Rewrite the postcard on another sheet of paper and make it more interesting for the reader by using more descriptive words.
■ Here are some words that might help you.

interesting	spacious	brilliant	large
pleasant	unfortunate	huge	fantastic
delicious	beautiful	tolerable	disappointing
excellent	chilly	first-class	yummy
comfortable	enormous	dreadful	reasonable
sad	ancient	scorching	amazing
	great	enjoyable	

■ Read your finished postcard to a partner, making it sound as interesting as you can. Can they spot the synonyms?

Name:

The impact of synonyms on audience

Tricky twins

■ Emily and Isabel are identical twins. They are even alike in what they are good at, so when their teacher has to write their reports at the end of the year she has a problem. How can she make their reports special for each of them?

■ The chart below shows the girls' progress in different subjects. In the 'Comments' columns, write down some words you could use when you write the girls' school reports, using synonyms for the words in bold type so that you can make the reports different.

Subject	Progress	Comments Emily	Comments Isabel
Literacy	Reading is **good**. Has got **much better**. Writing is improving but needs to work on spelling.		
Numeracy	**Quite good** at most things in maths. **Getting better** at division.		
Science	Understands new things. **Good** at experiments.		
ICT	**Very good**. Enjoys using the computer.		
Art	Drawing is **good** but painting and 3D work could **be better**.		
Music	Works **well** and sings **very well**.		
PE	**Not so good** at games but did **well** in gym and dance.		
History	Enjoyed working on the Romans and did some **good writing**.		
Geography	**Not very good** at understanding maps, but tries hard.		
Teacher's comment	**Really nice**. Very friendly and always tries her best. Helpful in class and works **very** hard.		

The impact of synonyms on audience

Taking a walk

■ You are going to write a list poem about a walk through a town. Below are some of the things you will write about on your walk. In each shape, write at least three synonyms you could use instead of the adjectives in bold.

A **noisy** road

An **old** building

A **big** tree

A **lovely** park

A **nice** garden

A **quiet** cat

■ Write a list poem below. Try each of your synonyms until you are sure you have chosen the one that sounds best.

I walked through town the other day and saw

_____

_____

_____

I walked through town the other day and heard

_____

_____

_____

I walked through town the other day and smelled

_____

_____

_____

Retelling a story in your own words

Objectives

To tell stories effectively and convey detailed information coherently for listeners. To show imagination through the language used to create emphasis, humour, atmosphere or suspense.

Background knowledge

Because children become familiar with particular books, DVDs and CDs, they often think that stories can only be told in one way. Being encouraged to retell well-known stories from the viewpoints of several characters makes it necessary to use the appropriate vocabulary. The three activities in this section do this by putting the children in roles from the tale 'The Three Little Pigs'. Many cultures have a rich oral storytelling tradition, where storytellers have their own version of the stories. If any of the children in your class are familiar with this culture, use their expertise to inform others.

Activities

In this section the children will try a variety of activities that help them to retell a story from a variety of viewpoints. They will need to consider the 'voice' and language use appropriate for each character's version of the story and the different text types used.

● **Photocopiable page 17 'How to capture a wolf'**
This activity focuses on antonyms. The children will see that using opposites completely alters the meaning of what is being conveyed. Explain that antonyms are words that mean the opposite of each other, such as *big* and *small*. Play a game asking for possible antonyms to words that you provide before completing the photocopiable sheet.

● **Photocopiable page 18 'The wolf's story'**
Before commencing the activity, put Big Bad Wolf into the hot-seat to provide the children with appropriate vocabulary and character voice. Highlight the need for the use of connectives, which in this case means that the wolf has to give reasons for his actions.
● **Photocopiable page 19 'Mother Pig's blog'**
Explain that a blog, short for weblog, is similar to a diary, but is written online so that lots of people can read it. Ask pairs of children to work together to complete the grid before writing the blog individually. Challenge more confident writers to extend their blog entries on the reverse of the sheet.

Further ideas

● **True stories:** Read *The True Story of the Three Little Pigs* by Jon Scieszka (Puffin). This acts as an example of how vocabulary changes when the story is told by a particular character and can be used in conjunction with photocopiable page 18 'The wolf's story'.
● **More instructions:** Encourage the children to develop their skills in writing instructions and explanations after using the photocopiable sheets, as they will have already been given a basis on which to structure each text type.
● **Blogs:** Invite the children to write a blog in role as one of the other characters in the story, changing their language accordingly.

What's on the CD-ROM

On the CD-ROM you will find:
● Printable versions of all three photocopiable pages.
● Answers to 'How to capture a wolf'.
● Interactive versions of 'How to capture a wolf' and 'Mother pig's blog'.

Retelling a story in your own words

How to capture a wolf

■ Following the successful capture of the Big Bad Wolf, the three little pigs wrote a set of instructions to help others with the same problem. Unfortunately, they got mixed up and wrote the opposite of what they meant!

■ Help them get it right by writing words that give the correct instructions. Write one or two suitable antonyms next to each word in bold. Try not to use the same word twice.

Wolves are very **dim** _____ so they are **easy** _____ to catch.

Things to remember:

- You should **always** _____ let the wolf into your house when he knocks on the door.

- It is a **good** _____ idea to build a house from straw, as the wolf will find it **difficult** _____ to blow down. If your house is made from bricks, the wolf will have an **effortless** _____ job.

- It is a **bad** _____ idea to tempt the wolf with food, as wolves are **rarely** _____ hungry.

Our worst _____ **idea**

1. Prepare a **small** _____ pot of **horrible** _____ -smelling food.

2. Put it **under** _____ a fire to cook, so that the **nasty** _____ cooking smells can go **down** _____ the chimney.

3. When the wolf notices the smell and climbs on to the roof, be very **noisy** _____ , so he **can** _____ hear you.

4. The wolf will be so **disappointed** _____ that he has found some food, that he will **unhurriedly** _____ climb down the chimney.

5. As he falls into your pot, **slowly** _____ put on the lid so that he **can** _____ escape.

Name:

Retelling a story in your own words

The wolf's story

After being captured by the three little pigs, Big Bad Wolf was taken away for questioning and asked to explain why he was trying to get the pigs and how he planned his attack.

■ Using the sentence starters below, imagine you are Big Bad Wolf and write your explanation. Make your explanation as clear as possible. You should use connectives that help you explain, such as **because**, **so**, **as**, **since** and **this caused**.

■ Start by explaining **why** he was after the pigs.

First, you should know that

_____

_____

■ Go on to explain **how** he carried out his plan.

I decided that I would need

_____

_____

I started by

_____

_____

After that,

_____

_____

The next thing

_____

_____

Finally,

_____

_____

Retelling a story in your own words

Mother Pig's blog

■ Imagine you are a worried Mother Pig, writing in your blog (weblog) about what happened when your three boys left home and the terrible events when the Big Bad Wolf came after them.

■ Begin by listing synonyms for the words in the boxes below, to show how she was feeling at different times in the week. How many of them can you use in your blog entries?

sad	worried	scared	happy

Monday _____

_____

_____

Tuesday _____

_____

_____

Wednesday _____

_____

_____

Thursday _____

_____

_____

Friday _____

_____

_____

Avoiding nice and said

Objectives

To explain how writers use expressive language to create atmosphere. To learn how to use a thesaurus effectively.

Background knowledge

The words *nice* and *said* are so common and learned at such a young age that we all use them without thinking. Children may not realise that the adjective *nice* has more than one meaning (it is synonymous with *pleasant*, *kind* and *good*, which all have slightly different meanings) and this has an impact on the choice of synonym for *nice* in different contexts. It will require a lot of practice and reinforcement for children to use more interesting alternatives before a wider vocabulary becomes automatic.

Activities

In this section the children will try a variety of activities that help them avoid using *nice* and *said* in formal and informal writing. They could consider how the level of formality affects word choice. Remind them that synonyms for each word cannot simply be substituted without considering the context of the sentence.

● **Photocopiable page 21 'Should zoos be banned?'**
If possible, read *Zoo* by Anthony Browne (Farrar, Straus and Giroux) before the activity to provide a context for the discussion text. Because some of the synonyms can be used in several places, the children will have to think carefully when choosing their words. Some words may be used more than once.

● **Photocopiable page 22 'But the sky is green!'**
Ask the children to use a thesaurus, work with a partner or use poster page 11 'Synonyms for said' for the first section of this activity. Children should avoid using synonyms more than once. Take care that the chosen words make sense in the context of the writing, for example, even though *asked* and *answered* are both synonyms for *said*, because they are opposites, they cannot be used as alternatives to each other.

● **Photocopiable page 23 'The new school'**
This activity offers another chance to use a thesaurus and an opportunity to reinforce the fact that synonyms do not always have exactly the same meanings. Before doing the activity, use ICT sessions to focus on email formats and the informality of the language usually used in them.

Further ideas

● **Guided reading:** Ask the children to look out for synonyms for *nice* and *said* during guided reading sessions, keeping a living list of the ones they find.

● **Acting the word:** In groups of three (one for each character), let the children rehearse and act out the scene from photocopiable page 22 'But the sky is green!', using the words they have selected in place of *said* to inform their delivery of the lines.

● **Don't use said:** Go to www.primaryresources.co.uk/english/pdfs/3said.pdf and share the poem 'Don't use said' with the class. Encourage them to learn it off by heart.

What's on the CD-ROM

On the CD-ROM you will find:
● Printable versions of all three photocopiable pages.
● Answers to 'Should zoos be banned?'.
● Interactive versions of 'But the sky is green!' and 'The new school'.

Avoiding nice and said

Should zoos be banned?

■ Make this piece more interesting by replacing the words in bold type with one from the box.

nice	said
appropriate pleasant happy enjoyable good	stated suggested told us believed claimed

Across the world, many people visit zoos for a (**nice**) _____

day out, but it is sometimes (**said**) _____ that zoos are a

bad thing; that they are not (**nice**) _____ places for wild

animals to be. However, it is also (**said**) _____ that zoos are

necessary, because they look after animals that might die out in the wild.

Zoo owners try to make life as (**nice**) _____ as they can

for the animals in their care. Most zoos provide (**nice**) _____

food that the animals will enjoy, and (**nice**) _____

environments for them to live in. Mr Green, a zoo owner, (**said**)

_____, "I look after my animals as well as I can." Mrs Bush,

a scientist, (**said**) _____ , "We have a breeding programme

at the zoo, to make sure endangered species do not become extinct. It is (**nice**)

_____ to know we are helping to keep animals alive."

However, some people think that it is not (**nice**) _____

for animals to be kept in cages. "It is wrong when wild animals do not live in their

natural environment," (**said**) _____ wildlife expert Nick Ellis.

He (**said**) _____ that many animals have unhappy lives in

zoos where they cannot do the things they would do in the wild.

What do *you* think?

Avoiding nice and said

But the sky is green!

■ How many synonyms can you find for the word **said**? List as many as you can in the box below.

[ ]

■ Choose words from your list to fill the empty boxes in the story extract below so it sounds interesting to the reader.

"Where are we?" [ ] James.

"I have no idea!" [ ] Sita.

"Look at the sky! It's green!" [ ] OJ.

Sita looked behind her. "I can still see the playground over there," she

[ ] . "That's weird!"

"Yes," [ ] James, "but listen – there's no sound."

"How did we get here?" OJ [ ] .

James quickly [ ] "Don't you remember? It was when you fell

against the gate in the playground!"

"Well, I didn't do it on purpose you know!" OJ [ ] angrily.

"OK, OK, no-one's saying you did," [ ] Sita, trying to calm things

down a bit. "The question is," she [ ] "can we get back?"

James thought for a moment, then [ ] "Maybe we shouldn't rush

to get back. Maybe we should explore a bit first."

Sita and OJ exchanged nervous glances. "I'm not sure," OJ [ ] .

"Me neither," [ ] Sita, nervously.

Avoiding nice and said

The new school

■ How many words can you find to use instead of **nice**? List as many as you can in the box below.

■ Choose words from your list to use instead of **nice** to make the email below more interesting.

To	andi@email.com
cc	
Subject	New school

Hi Andi,

Well! We're here! Our new house is really _____ and my room has

a _____ view, looking over the fields at the back. However,

I have to tell you about my new school! It's really, really _____!

I was a bit worried, as we always had such a _____ time

at the old place, but I tell you, it's _____! There are some

quite _____ kids in my class and one called Charley who's

really _____. When you come to stay I know we'll have a

_____ time together. The teacher, Mrs Smudgen, I'm not so sure

about yet. She's one of those people who has a _____ smile,

but you can't really tell what she's thinking, if you know what I mean! But,

there's some really _____ stuff to do around the playground,

like adventure climbing frames and a _____ field and loads of

_____ games marked on the playground. Email back soon! Hope

you're having a _____ time without me!

Chris

Words related to everyday life

Objectives

To identify how talk varies with purpose. To show imagination through the language used to create emphasis, humour, atmosphere or suspense.

Background knowledge

Our knowledge of language is based around our everyday lives, with particular vocabularies being relevant to each situation. While individual circumstances differ, many elements are common to us all. Such familiarity can make us lazy with language, as we become used to using a limited vocabulary. However, we can use this shared knowledge as a basis for extending everyday vocabulary so that even ordinary situations can be brought to life through interesting and appropriate word choices.

Activities

In this section familiar situations provide the context for children to give careful consideration to word choices, going beyond those most commonly used.

● **Photocopiable page 25 'The swimming pool'**
Without spending time discussing and capturing interesting ideas, children may write only the more obvious options. Ask: *What happens at swimming pools apart from swimming?* Let the children mime activities for others to guess. Ask: *What sort of conversations do people have there? How are they different depending on the people involved and the situation?*

● **Photocopiable page 26 'The park in autumn'**
Ideally, go to the park or go on a 'senses walk' in the school grounds before starting this activity. Tell the children to work in four groups, one for each of the senses used, then share their results for everyone to use (some boxes on the grid will remain empty).

● **Photocopiable page 27 'The supermarket'**
In real life, parent–child conversations can be very perfunctory, so modelling some scenarios would be a good idea. Draw attention to the different 'voice' of the two characters. Before completing the activity, ask pairs of children to act out the conversations that might happen between a parent/guardian and a child as they go shopping.

Further ideas

● **Autumn display:** Ask the children to write words on leaf shapes to describe what they saw, heard and felt on an autumn walk. Ask for synonyms for words such as *beautiful*, *crunchy* and *cold*. Display the leaves on the outline of a tree skeleton.

● **Supermarket cards:** Give pairs of children cards with phrases printed on them as prompts, for example: buying vegetables, meeting a friend, choosing bread, asking where to find something, deciding which cake to buy, at the checkout. Use the cards as prompts to an improvised conversation.

● **Mini thesaurus:** Let the children make their own mini thesauruses, or provide illustrated contributions to a class thesaurus.

● **Poetry archive:** Explore more poetry about everyday life. Visit the website www.poetryarchive.org/ to search for poems, information about poets and poetic forms.

What's on the CD-ROM

On the CD-ROM you will find:
● Printable versions of all three photocopiable pages.
● Interactive version of 'The park in autumn'.

Words related to everyday life

The swimming pool

■ Imagine you are at a busy swimming pool. Use your senses to find words you could use to describe what is happening around you.

I can see...

I can hear...

I can feel...

I can smell...

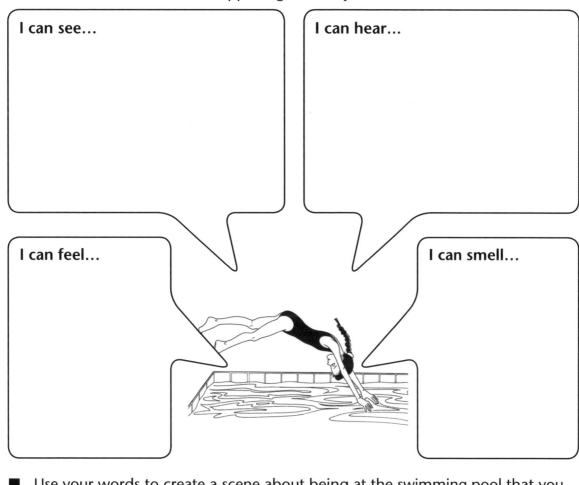

■ Use your words to create a scene about being at the swimming pool that you can act out, such as a conversation between two friends. What do they say to each other? Write the dialogue here. Continue on another sheet if you need to.

_____

_____

_____

_____

_____

_____

_____

Illustrations © 2010, Catherine Ward.

Name:

The park in autumn

■ Imagine you are visiting a park in the autumn. In the grid below, write some words and phrases to describe the scene. There are a few examples to get you started. (You will not be able to fill in all of the boxes.)

	I can see	I can feel	I can hear	I can smell
People	Children biking Adults talking			
Trees			Crunchy leaves rustling	
The sky				
Animals				A wet dog
The weather		The rain		

■ Use some of your ideas to write a non-rhyming poem. One has been started below, continue it on another sheet of paper.

What's happening at the park?

Children on bikes are zooming, their brakes squealing,

A wet dog brushes against my legs,

Words related to everyday life

The supermarket

■ Write a conversation between a parent and child as they do their shopping at the supermarket. What might they say about:

- the different things they buy, such as food, household goods, pet food and toiletries
- how much they need of things such as fruit, vegetables, milk, meat and bread
- special offers they find
- other shoppers and people they might know who are also shopping.

Mother	Child

Illustrations © 2010, Catherine Ward.

■ Act out your conversation with a partner. Can you add to the dialogue, using this conversation as a starter?

Assessment

The following grid shows the main objectives and activities covered in this chapter. You can use the grid to locate activities that cover a particular focus that you are keen to monitor.

Objective	Page	Activity title
To understand the term *synonym*.	13 14 15	Holiday postcard Tricky twins Taking a walk
To use synonyms in writing.	13 14 15	Holiday postcard Tricky twins Taking a walk
To tell stories effectively and convey detailed information coherently for listeners.	18	The wolf's story
To show imagination through the language used to create emphasis, humour, atmosphere or suspense.	17 18 19 25 26	How to capture a wolf The wolf's story Mother Pig's blog The swimming pool The park in autumn
To explain how writers use expressive language to create atmosphere.	21 22	Should zoos be banned? But the sky is green!
To learn how to use a thesaurus effectively.	22 23	But the sky is green! The new school
To identify how talk varies with purpose.	27	The supermarket

Observation and record keeping

Keep a note of those children who easily offer suggestions, as well as those who have fewer ideas, to plan for further work where necessary. Be alert to children using words that you have worked on in everyday conversations, praising them. Make sure writing tasks give children the opportunity to use synonyms and appropriate character voices. If you are focusing on specific words, such as synonyms for *nice*, *said*, *big* and *fun*, keep a class tick list and tick when children use alternatives. Encourage the children to keep their own record of synonyms they have used.

Assessment activity

● **What you need**
Photocopiable page 29 'Spy report'.
● **What to do**
Ask pairs of children to act out the suspects making their plans. Explain the task, pointing out that one is formal writing and the other is informal, so this will affect the words they choose. Remind the children about using synonyms for *said*.

Differentiation

● Let less confident writers draw Igor and write his words to his boss and Nadia in speech bubbles.
● Encourage more confident writers to use speech marks correctly and use their completed writing as the basis for a short scripted scene.

Further learning

● **Writing:** Most synonyms can be used with any subsequent writing. Children should be reminded to use their personal bank so that synonyms become embedded and automatic. Tell the children to think of everyday words that might be used for a piece of writing and ask for suggestions for suitable alternatives.
● **Across the curriculum:** Because of the cross-curricular nature of language, there will be opportunities for using newly learned synonyms in a range of subject areas. Children should be reminded of this so that their learning is transferred and therefore reinforced. You should model this explicitly in the language you use with your class.

Assessment

Spy report

■ Igor the spy has been spying on two suspects who are plotting to steal a secret formula. He used a secret CCTV camera to watch and hear their conversation as they discussed how they would sneak into the laboratory where the secret formula was being made, find it and escape.

■ What would Igor write in his official report to his boss and what would he put in an email to his friend Nadia, another spy who knew about the suspects?

What the suspects said	What Igor wrote in his email to Nadia	What Igor wrote in his report to his boss

Word of the week

The Word of the week pages provide information on one word linked to each section in the chapter. Each word is described in some of the following categories: word definition, word origin, word family, alternative words, fascinating facts and activities. Not all categories are relevant to every word.

You can use the words as a focus to support your work on the different sections of the chapter. For example, you could create a display around it. The information is a starting point for a word focus. The words could form part of your classroom living word bank.

You could also use the word of the week as a springboard to inspire children to think about or research fascinating facts about words, find interesting quotations and to encourage them to use dictionaries and thesauruses.

Extremely

- **Word definition:** An adverb which means very or exceedingly. It is a useful synonym for two commonly over-used words: *very* and *really*.
- **Word origin:** From the Latin *extremus*, meaning the outermost or utmost.
- **Word family:** Noun and adjective: *extreme*.
- **Alternative words:** Exceedingly, exceptionally, greatly, especially, highly, notably.
- **Fascinating facts:** It can be used to describe opposites, such as *extremely happy* or *extremely sad*. Challenge the children to see how many pairs of antonyms they can list that can be preceded by the word *extremely*.
- **Activities:** In geography, describe places as being *extremely dry*, *flat, mountainous or remote*. In history, describe the Greeks as being *extremely civilised* or the Roman army as being *extremely well organised*.

> Linked section:
> The impact of synonyms on audience, page 12

Imagination

- **Word definition:** A noun which means to be able to form pictures in the mind of things not present.
- **Word origin:** From the Latin *imago* meaning image or likeness.
- **Word family:** Noun and verb: *image*; verb: *imagine*; adjective: *imaginary*.
- **Alternative words:** Fantasy, creative thought, vision.
- **Fascinating facts:** Albert Einstein said 'I am enough of an artist to draw freely upon my imagination. Imagination is more important than knowledge. Knowledge is limited. Imagination encircles the world.'
- **Activities:** When working in literacy on 'imaginary worlds', ask the children to explain in words, pictures or music, what *imagination* means to them. Are there common elements? What differences are there? Use images, music or words as stimuli to harnessing the imagination. Play John Lennon's *Imagine*, or La Toya Jackson's (1986) or Tamia's (1998) recordings of *Imagination*. Make a collection of images of imaginary creatures, such as mermaids, unicorns, cyclops, dragons or aliens.

> Linked section:
> Retelling a story in your own words, page 16

Delightful

- **Word definition:** An adjective meaning very pleasant or charming. A synonym for *nice* in the context of *greatly pleasing*. Literally meaning *full of delight*, children will need reminding to drop the second 'l' when spelling the word.
- **Word origin:** From Latin origin, *delectare*, meaning alluring or charming.
- **Word family:** Noun and verb: *delight.*
- **Alternative words:** Agreeable, attractive, fascinating, lovely, pleasing.
- **Fascinating facts:** The biblical name *Saphir* means delightful.
- **Activities:** Encourage the children to have fun illustrating delightful food or a delightful holiday location. Ask: *What makes a delightful person?* Let the children annotate a drawing, noting the features they have selected. Reinforce the word in everyday interactions, by saying, for example, *Thank you, that was a delightful thing to do.*

> **Linked section:** Avoiding nice and said, page 20

Conversation

- **Word definition:** A noun meaning to talk and exchange ideas.
- **Word origin:** Latin root *conversatio* meaning to converse.
- **Word family:** Noun and verb: *converse*; adjective: *conversant.*
- **Alternative words:** Chat, comment, communicate, talk, gossip, exchange.
- **Fascinating facts:** This word developed into a whole movement in 18th century Italy where people would gather to talk about artistic or intellectual topics, in what became known as a *conversazione*. Recreate this idea by creating a space for a 'conversation cafe' where children meet at suitable times for conversation. Post a 'Topic of the day', which they must discuss to avoid it degenerating into chat.
- **Activities:** Play the game 'What are they thinking?' where one child adopts a particular pose or stance and pairs of children have a conversation about what that person might be thinking. Players may also ask the person yes/no questions.

> **Linked section:** Words related to everyday life, page 24

Fun with words

Children need many opportunities to use alternatives for commonly-used words before they become a part of their personal vocabulary bank. Playing games and consciously reinforcing new words in everyday situations helps this hard-wiring process. The ideas below offer some examples of how to reinforce topics covered in this chapter.

Circle game
● Pass a series of objects around the circle. Each child has to say something different or use different words to describe it. Change to a new object when words are clearly hard to find and start again in a different part of the circle.

Characters
● Prepare a set of character cards, such as *a sad clown, an old woman, a nervous child, a wise man, an angry person, an artist, a doctor, a gardener* and *a footballer*. Give the class a situation, such as *making a phone call to a friend, giving directions to find a place, making a hairdresser's appointment* and *telling someone about your recent holiday or something you have bought*. Working in groups, ask the children place the pack of cards face down in the centre of the table taking turns to pick a card. They must say a few sentences in role as the person on the card in the given situation.

Synonyms
● Help the children to become familiar with a wider spoken-vocabulary by using synonyms for *said* and *nice*, for example: *What a **beautiful** piece of handwriting; Thank you for being so **thoughtful** when your friend was upset; Jack **explained** why he chose that method.*

Alternatives
● Prepare a story where you have overused a commonly used word, such as *fun, big, nice* or *scared*. Arrange the class in mixed-ability teams. As you read the story to the class, they have to stand up every time one of the words is said, but only if they can suggest an alternative that would fit the story, winning a point for a correct word, but losing one if it has already been used. You could add a point if they can also spell the word. You may need a referee to spot who stands up first.

The antonym wall
● Put large pieces of paper on the wall. Challenge the children to fill the paper by the end of the day or week with as many words as possible together with their opposites. Encourage them to use dictionaries to check their spelling but emphasise that this is not a spelling activity. This could be a team game, each team having a different coloured pen to use. As the list grows, children have to check to see they are not repeating words already used, although synonyms are allowed.

Chapter 2
Word origins

Introduction

The English language we use today is the result of many influences over hundreds of years, making English a fascinating language to study. The patterns that children can see in prefixes, for example, can help them to understand word meanings and help their spelling. They will discover some of the influences that other languages have had on our own. However, language does not stand still, so there are opportunities for children to investigate our changing language and even invent some new words of their own.

Poster notes

Latin prefixes (page 34)

The poster provides words that have 'grown' from the prefix, which is at its root. While some of the words will be familiar to the children, they may not know their origins, so discussions starting with these words will help to reinforce the meaning of the word origins, and help them to work out the meanings of those words that are less familiar. For example: *What does the 'bi' part of* bicycle *or* binoculars *refer to?* Having deduced that, can the children work out what *bilingual* means? As all of the prefixes are of Latin origin, a link can be made to the influence of the Roman invasion on our present-day language.

In this chapter

Interesting and unusual prefixes page 35	To use a knowledge of prefixes to develop understanding of word meanings.
Foreign word roots page 39	To use a knowledge of word origins to develop an understanding of word meanings. To be aware of the influence of other languages on English.
Old and new words page 43	To realise that vocabulary changes over time and to discuss why this happens.
Nonsense words page 47	To use knowledge of word meanings and origins to write meanings for invented words. To use knowledge of prefixes and word roots to invent new words in context. To demonstrate an understanding of word derivations.
Assessment page 51	Activities and ideas to assess children's understanding of word origins and related meanings.

Word origins

LATIN PREFIXES

bi = two

binoculars
biped
bilingual
binary
bicycle

inter = between

interpret
interchange
interrogate
international
intercept

circum = round

circus
circumference
circular
circumstance
circumnavigate

anti = against

antifreeze
antipodes
antiseptic
antidote
antibiotic

contra = against

contrast
contract
contradict
contrary
contraband

Illustrations © 2010, Catherine Ward.

PHOTOCOPIABLE

Interesting and unusual prefixes

Objective

To use a knowledge of prefixes to develop understanding of word meanings.

Background knowledge

Prefixes are placed in front of a word to add to or change its meaning. Children will already be familiar with prefixes such as 'un-' changing, for example *do* to *undo*; or 'im-' changing *possible* to *impossible*. Such knowledge can help them to work out the meanings of unfamiliar words and help with their spelling. A range of dictionaries will be a useful starting point, but children need to realise that, for example, not every word that begins with 'inter-' is using it as a prefix, such as *interior* or *internal*. For this, they will have to read the word definitions as well as using the dictionaries for finding words.

Activities

In this section, children are introduced to a range of prefixes that may be less familiar to them – indeed, they are unlikely to be aware of them as prefixes, particularly the prefix 'super-'. Knowing the meaning of the word *super* will help children to easily deduce the meanings of words where it is used as a prefix.

● **Photocopiable page 36 'Superhero to the rescue!'**
Let the children start this activity using words they know, before being challenged to discover new words by using dictionaries. You will need to discuss ideas for the problem the superhero might be tackling, such as saving someone from a burning building. As they are only writing the opening frame, children do not need to plan the whole story, although this could be used as a follow-up activity.

● **Photocopiable page 37 'Aerotrans: air transport for the world'**
Point out the difference in spelling between *aero* and *air*, perhaps using the words *aeroplane* and *airplane* as examples (*airplane* is more commonly used in the US). Why do the children think the chocolate bar *Aero* is called this? Have dictionaries available for the children to use.

● **Photocopiable page 38 'Word shapes'**
This activity provides another opportunity for the children to discover new words using dictionaries. Show the children several examples of calligrams or shape poems on the board before they try creating their own. You will be able to find examples through an internet search, which can be shared on the interactive whiteboard.

Further ideas

● **Word hunt:** Tell the children to find words with prefixes in their reading and add them to a class collection. Challenge them to use these words in their writing.
● **Superhero on film:** Watch a cartoon clip of a superhero and list his or her superpowers (copyright permitting).
● **Calligram display:** Ask the children to select their best calligram to create in a large form, using colour, for a whole-class display.

What's on the CD-ROM

On the CD-ROM you will find:
● Printable versions of all three photocopiable pages.
● Interactive versions of 'Superhero to the rescue!' and 'Word shapes'.

Name:

Interesting and unusual prefixes

Superhero to the rescue!

■ Write words you could use to describe your own superhero using the prefixes below. Some words are provided to start you off.

super- (greater, or better than)	auto- (self)	tele- (far off)	aero- (air)
superhuman	automaton	teleport	aerodynamic

■ Use as many of these words as you can to create the opening frame of a comic strip where your superhero saves the day. Put some words in speech bubbles and some in the text box underneath.

Aerotrans: air transport for the world

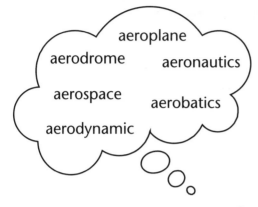

aeroplane

aerodrome   aeronautics

aerospace   aerobatics

aerodynamic

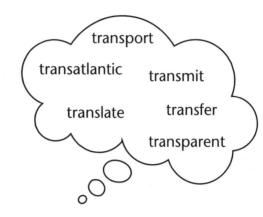

transport

transatlantic   transmit

translate   transfer

transparent

aero- means **air**   **trans**- means **across**

■   Use as many of the words in the bubbles as you can in an advert for Aerotrans'
new aeroplane. What can it do? Where does it fly? Why is it better than other
planes? How can you persuade people to travel on it?

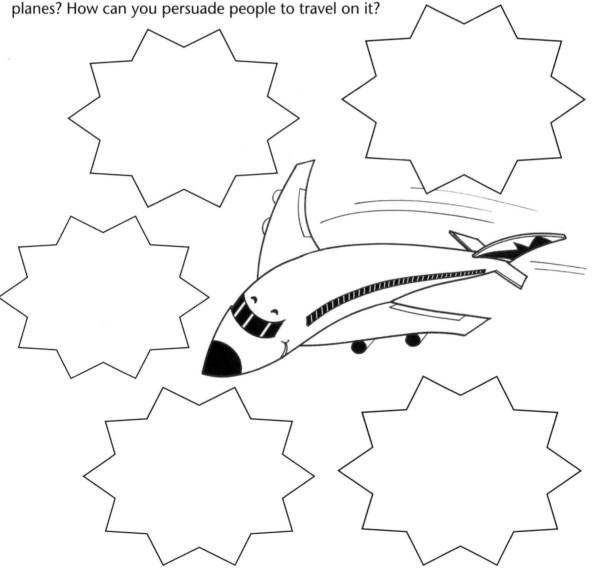

Illustrations © 2010, Catherine Ward.

Name:

Interesting and unusual prefixes

Word shapes

■ Here are some prefixes and their meanings. Use a dictionary to find and list some words with these prefixes.

micro- (small)	anti- (against)	inter- (between)	contra- (against)

■ Choose some of your words to write as calligrams. Calligrams are poems that use words as if they were shapes, so you can picture what the word means. How many of your own can you make? For example:

The caterpillar was s l o w l y getting **bigger** and **bigger**

_____

_____

_____

_____

_____

_____

_____

PHOTOCOPIABLE ■SCHOLASTIC

Foreign word roots

To use knowledge of word origins to develop an understanding of word meanings. To be aware of the influence of other languages on English.

Background knowledge

Children may not be aware of the influences that invaders and settlers of the past have had on our language. Many English words have Latin or Greek roots and there are literally thousands of words that began as French, reflecting the lasting influence of the Norman invasion. For example, virtually all words ending in '-tion', '-ible' and '-able' were originally French. Try it out – *information, possible, agreeable* – it works.

Activities

This section offers children the chance to investigate everyday words that have come to us from other languages in the distant and near past. It can be linked with work on Greeks or Romans in history, or with French as a modern foreign language.

● **Photocopiable page 40 'Word archaeologists'**
Point out that while most of the roots in the activity are prefixes, '-graph', '-scope' and '-phone' are suffixes, coming at the ends of words, so dictionaries can only help to check spellings. *Octo* is the Latin spelling of the original Greek *okto*, but is given in the Latin form here to help children with their spelling.

● **Photocopiable page 41 'International menu'**
Investigating food words illustrates that there are now even wider international influences on our language. Encourage the children to use their own experience to complete some of the activity, but also use other sources, such as books from the school library, an internet search or an online dictionary such as dictionary.reference.com. *The Oxford School Dictionary of Word Origins* is an extremely useful source for investigating word derivations of all kinds.

● **Photocopiable page 42 'Everyday French'**
Rhyming dictionaries are useful for this activity. You should be flexible about the metre or rhythm in the poems that the children write – the occasional syllable or two can be overlooked.

Further ideas

● **Food fun:** Ask the children to bring in packaging, photographs or adverts that illustrate the use of foreign food words for discussion and display.
● **How do you say that?:** Using the French/English words that have been discovered, ask the children to pronounce the words with a French accent. This fun activity will help them to realise that the French language has massively influenced English and that they know more French words than they realised. This will provide reinforcement for the words they have been using, focusing particularly on the final syllable/root, which will also help with spelling.

What's on the CD-ROM

On the CD-ROM you will find:
● Printable versions of all three photocopiable pages.
● Answers to 'International menu'.
● Interactive versions of 'Word archaeologists' and 'International menu'.

Name:

Foreign word roots

Word archaeologists

■ Can you uncover words from the past? You may have to dig deep into the pages of a dictionary to find them. These words all have Greek roots, from the time when the Greeks were the most important nation in Europe. Use the clues to list words that fit the root.

geo- (earth)	micro- (small)	octo- (eight)	tele- (far-off)
geography			
-phone (to speak)	**-scope** (to look at)	**-graph** (to write)	**deca-** (ten)

■ Use the words you have found in sentences. For example:

Geography is the study of the Earth.

_____

_____

_____

_____

PHOTOCOPIABLE   ■SCHOLASTIC
www.scholastic.co.uk

Foreign word roots

International menu

■ Esperanto's international restaurant serves dishes from many parts of the world. Use a variety of sources to find out which countries the items on the menu come from.

Food	Origin
taramasalata	
spaghetti Bolognese	
gateau	
chapatti	
sushi	
yoghurt	
pizza	
fajita	
baguette	
Gorgonzola	
meringue	
tagliatelle	
hummus	
risotto	
broccoli	
taco	

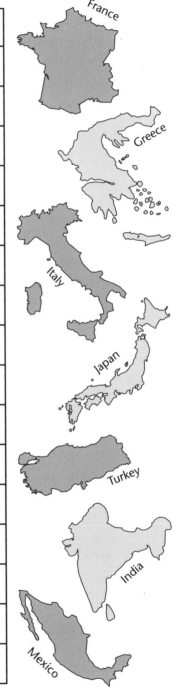

Arabia (Arabic)   France   India (Hindi)   Italy   Japan

Greece   Mexico (Mexican Spanish)   Turkey

Illustration © 2010, Nova Development.

Name:

Everyday French

■ Did you know that you use loads of French words every day? Almost all our words ending in **-tion** and **-ible** were originally French. They are just pronounced differently. How many can you think of?

Words ending in **-tion**	Words ending in **-ible**

■ Now choose some of your words to write a poem in rhyming couplets about words. One has been started as an example.

Words

Words can give an explanation
Words can reach an entire nation
Words can make things possible
Or incomprehensible!

_____

_____

_____

_____

_____

_____

_____

_____

_____

Old and new words

To realise that vocabulary changes over time and to discuss why this happens.

Background knowledge

The *Oxford English Dictionary* estimates that there are about 250,000 English words. About 20 per cent of these are no longer in use. It is hard to imagine a time when all the words we know today were first coined – we do tend to take language for granted. However, whenever there is a new discovery or invention, we need a new word for it and we begin to realise how our language is constantly developing. In the same way, as things change and move on, so other words die out.

Activities

The activities in this section will draw the children's attention to the idea of our changing language, helping them to realise that while some words go out of everyday use, others soon fill their place, so that our language is regenerating all the time. Talk about the influence of technology on language as an example of this.

● **Photocopiable page 44 'A blast from the past'**
Give the children the chance to read the words on the photocopiable sheet aloud, playing with their sounds. Before the activity, ask the children to think about how different the experience would have been 300 years ago. Have a class discussion about who your character is, where they are travelling to, why, how they are getting there and how long it might take.

● **Photocopiable page 45 'Shakespeare's inventions'**
Suggest using compound words, as Shakespeare often did, for those finding it hard to start. The definitions, for which the children are asked to make new words, have been chosen to make use of all the senses. Use the first example to generate other possibilities before letting the children work on their own ideas for the rest of the activity.

● **Photocopiable page 46 'Technospeak'**
This activity looks at 21st century language. Note that most of the words are linked to new technologies and are often more associated with young people. When they have completed the activity, ask the children to explain their choices, saying how they knew that the words they chose are new.

Further ideas

● **Technotalk:** Discuss the impact of technology on language and how this has happened throughout history. Using knowledge the children have from a historical period you have studied, ask them to write a first-person passage on a particular topic, using appropriate language that reflects the time.
● **Drawing rooms:** Draw and annotate pictures of rooms and fashions from periods in the past to illustrate words (most of them nouns) no longer used.
● **Will's words:** Find out more about Shakespeare's influences on English at: shakespeare.about.com

 **What's on the CD-ROM**

On the CD-ROM you will find:
● Printable versions of all three photocopiable pages.
● Answers to 'Technospeak'.
● Interactive versions of 'A blast from the past' and 'Technospeak'.

Name:

Old and new words

A blast from the past

■ Here are some old-fashioned words that we do not use any more.

apace – quickly
backarapper – firework
coney – rabbit
daffadowndilly – daffodil
fubsy – short and fat
fopdoodle – fool

jeepers-creepers – wow
malison – a curse
nappiness – having a nap
niddering – cowardly
skirr – a whirring, grating noise
traveltainted – tired after travelling

■ Use as many of these words as you can to write as someone living 300 years ago about a journey you have taken. Write about who and what you saw, what you heard and how you felt.

What a journey I had!

_____

_____

_____

_____

_____

_____

_____

_____

_____

_____

Illustrations © 2010, Catherine Ward.

Old and new words

Shakespeare's inventions

■ Famous playwright William Shakespeare invented more than 3000 words. Some did not survive, but we still use more than 1200 of them today. Here are some of the words he is thought to have used for the first time.

moonbeam

bedroom

eyeball

champion

zany

outbreak

■ Notice how many of these are compound words. Try making up your own new words to describe the phrases below. The first one is done to help you (though you may think of a better one!).

Phrase	My new word
When you are just going to sleep.	fallslooping
The smell of delicious cooking.	
The noise of birds quarrelling.	
The soft, warm, furry touch of a cat.	
A shiny, polished floor.	
The sharp taste of a sour lemon.	
The excitement of waking up on your birthday.	
How you feel when it thunders.	
The sound of breaking glass.	
A clear, starry night sky.	

Illustrations © 2010, Catherine Ward.

Old and new words

Technospeak

■ Highlight the 21st century words in this blog (weblog).

My friend texted me and asked if I wanted to go to hers for a sleepover at the weekend. Wicked! I thought. I'll wear lots of bling and my new hoodie. She said we'd sleep in and have brunch instead of breakfast and asked if I wanted my meal supersizing.

My mum keeps going on at me, calling me a mouse potato 'cos I'm on my laptop so much. What a stress puppy she is! Now we've got WiFi in the house I can go online anywhere. It's great. My mum needs to get herself upskilled, I tell you, she has no idea about technology. She has to get me to help her with emails!

Mind you, she did manage to work out how to use her new mobile, eventually, with a bit of help from me. I got her fixed up with a great ringtone that I downloaded from the net. It was a song she likes to do karaoke to. Actually, it's not bad. I even put it on my MP3 player! But don't tell her, will you?! (There's no chance she'll read this blog!)

PHOTOCOPIABLE   **SCHOLASTIC**
www.scholastic.co.uk

Nonsense words

To use knowledge of word meanings and origins to write meanings for invented words. To use knowledge of prefixes and word roots to invent new words in context. To demonstrate an understanding of word derivations.

Background knowledge

Many words coined by Edward Lear and Lewis Carroll are complete nonsense, with no reference to existing words, but interestingly because the grammar and syntax follow accepted rules, we somehow have at least some understanding of what is being said. Other nonsense words do include parts of words, offering some clues to their meaning. When children invent their own words using these conventions it helps them to focus on word parts and their meanings.

Activities

In this section, the children will be able to make use of the prefixes and root words they have been working with, to have some fun inventing words of their own that may sound like pure nonsense, but do have an identifiable derivation.

● **Photocopiable page 48 'Autosupergraphophone!'**
It is worth revising the various affixes already covered before you start this activity. Help the children who are put off by the long words to break the words into chunks for easier decoding. Share some book blurbs beforehand as examples of writing style.

● **Photocopiable page 49 'Make your own words'**
The words provided for this activity include some of the prefixes and suffixes that the children have already worked on. They should use these to create their own new words, which they should be able to give a sensible meaning for.

● **Photocopiable page 50 'A new discovery'**
This activity is not as far-fetched as it may seem. New creatures are being discovered every year, especially in remote forest regions, such as Borneo or in the depths of Guyana, which has the least studied rainforest containing newly discovered giant otters and arachnids. Many explorers in the past gave us the names of creatures we know well today. Use poster page 34 'Prefixes' as a prompt.

Further ideas

● **Mr Carroll and Mr Lear:** Read some of Lewis Carroll's and Edward Lear's poetry to illustrate nonsense words.
● **Root dominoes:** Make sets of cards with prefixes, suffixes and other parts of words. Cards are dealt in the same way as dominoes. Players take turns to place cards side-by-side to see what new words they can make. They should record the words as they go and choose definitions for any new words they create.
● **Latin creatures:** Challenge more confident readers to investigate generic and specific Latin names for animals. What connections can they find?
● **How I got my name:** Find out about how some species' names came about. Some modern scientists have a sense of humour, such as the scientist who named two new cicada species *B. laureli* and *B. hardyi*.

What's on the CD-ROM

On the CD-ROM you will find:
● Printable versions of all three photocopiable pages.

Name:

Nonsense words

Autosupergraphophone!

■ Here are some nonsense words made from prefixes and word roots. Can you work out what they mean?

Word	Meaning
superphone	
transaeromobile	
octoscope	
contrasuperisation	
transgeograph	

■ Use these new words to write a blurb for a new science-fiction book for children. The meanings you have chosen for your words will help you to decide what the book is about.

PHOTOCOPIABLE

■ SCHOLASTIC
www.scholastic.co.uk

Nonsense words

Make your own words

■ Look closely at the words at the bottom of the page. They are all made from smaller words, such as **auto** + **route** = **autoroute**

■ Cut the words into these smaller parts, then try putting them together in different ways to make new words. Write your new words in the space below and give a definition for each of them. You can read your questions and answers to make it sound like a poem. An example is given to help you.

What is a...?	It's...
Microroute	A path that insects make through the jungle.

✂ -

micrometer	teleport	periscope
international	transatlantic	contraband
aeroplane	autoroute	megaphone

Name:

Nonsense words

A new discovery

■ Use your knowledge of prefixes and word roots to describe a newly discovered creature, maybe an insect or an animal from the densest jungle or deepest ocean. What will you call it?

■ Write an entry for an online encyclopedia about your creature. Invent names for parts of its body and explain how it makes use of them. For example, it might have superskin that it uses as armour against predators or microvision for its hundreds of tiny eyes. Add some fascinating facts about the creature's behaviour.

Creaturepedia's amazing animals

Name of creature: _____

Description: _____

_____

_____

_____

Typical behaviour: _____

_____

_____

_____

Habitat: _____

_____

_____

_____

Fascinating facts: _____

_____

_____

_____

Assessment

The following grid shows the main objectives and activities covered in this chapter. You can use the grid to locate activities that cover a particular focus that you are keen to monitor.

Objective	Page	Activity title
To use a knowledge of prefixes to develop understanding of word meanings.	36 37 38	Superhero to the rescue! Aerotrans: air transport for the world Word shapes
To use a knowledge of word origins to develop an understanding of word meanings.	40	Word archaeologists
To be aware of the influence of other languages on English.	40 41 42	Word archaeologists International menu Everyday French
To realise that vocabulary changes over time and to discuss why this happens.	44 45 46	A blast from the past Shakespeare's inventions Technospeak
To use knowledge of word meanings and origins to write meanings for invented words.	48 49 50	Autosupergraphophone! Make your own words A new discovery
To use knowledge of prefixes and word roots to invent new words in context.	49 50	Make your own words A new discovery
To demonstrate an understanding of word derivations.	48 49 50	Autosupergraphophone! Make your own words A new discovery

Observation and record keeping

Make an *I can* book including the learning objectives written in child-friendly language. Let the children record how well they think they have done using smiley, straight or sad faces beside each objective. Record your opinion in a second box. For your own records, use a traffic light system on a class list where levels of attainment are recorded against each learning objective.

Assessment activity

● **What you need**
Photocopiable page 52 'Dictionary'.
● **What to do**
Explain that because language changes, dictionaries are always being updated. The children should use their learning about parts of words to write their own definitions of the words on the sheet. Some have word roots they know but others can be left to their imagination.

Differentiation

● Encourage less confident learners to work with an adult who reads the words out to them, breaking the words down into parts.
● Challenge more confident learners to use some of the words in a piece of writing that is appropriate to the definition of the word.

Further learning

● **Advert:** Ask each child to select one word from the assessment activity for an advertising campaign for a new product and design an advert for it.
● **Guided reading:** Encourage the children to collect and define words containing prefixes and suffixes to build up their own mini-dictionary of words they have read in context.

Name:

Dictionary

■ Imagine your job is to update dictionaries. Here is a list of some words that you have to write the definitions for. How will you explain them in the next edition of your dictionary?

New word	Definition
autowalker	
clacket	
superscope	
microgetti	
aeroblog	
antioctomobile	
prattle basket	
fourses	
transbritish	

Word of the week

The Word of the week pages provide information on one word linked to each section in the chapter. Each word is described in some of the following categories: word definition, word origin, word family, alternative words, fascinating facts and activities. Not all categories are relevant to every word.

You can use the words as a focus to support your work on the different sections of the chapter. For example, you could create a display around it. The information is a starting point for a word focus. The words could form part of your classroom living word bank.

You could also use the word of the week as a springboard to inspire children to think about or research fascinating facts about words, find interesting quotations and to encourage them to use dictionaries and thesauruses.

Definition

- **Word definition:** A noun which means an explanation of a word or a phrase's meaning.
- **Word origin:** From the Latin *definire* which means to define.
- **Word family:** Verb: *define.*
- **Alternative words:** Explanation, meaning, classification.
- **Fascinating facts:** Dictionaries used to be ordered by group – for example all the animals would be listed together. The first reliable English dictionary as we know them today was written by Samuel Johnson in 1755 and called *A dictionary of the English Language.*
- **Activities:** Play a game where you read definitions from a classroom dictionary for teams of children to decide on the probable words. Give points both for guessing the correct word and for spelling it correctly.

> **Linked section:**
> Interesting and unusual prefixes, page 35

Petrified

- **Word definition:** A verb which means to turn to stone or to frighten. To be petrified literally means to be so scared that you cannot move.
- **Word origin:** From the Greek *petra*, meaning rock.
- **Word family:** Verb: *petrify.*
- **Alternative words:** Frozen, anxious, fearful, dazed.
- **Fascinating facts:** Petrification is the process that occurs to make fossils from organic materials, such as wood.
- **Activities:** Using freeze-framing in drama is an excellent way to help children to remember the word. Ask the children to write poems describing how they felt at a time when they were so scared that they were petrified. Or use a character in a book, film or television programme that has had a terrifying experience. Read Anthony Browne's *The Tunnel* (Walker Books), where the boy is turned to stone and his sister's love brings him back to life. Encourage the children to ask their own questions about the story as a basis for discussion.

> **Linked section:**
> Foreign word roots, page 39

Era

- **Word definition:** A noun meaning a period in history.
- **Word origin:** From ancient Rome where tokens called *aera* were used for counting and it has come to mean 'counting a period of time'.
- **Alternative words:** Age, period, generation, cycle.
- **Fascinating facts:** The Mesozoic era was roughly 180–251 million years ago. It was the time of the dinosaurs and included the Triassic, Jurassic and Cretaceous period.
- **Activities:** When looking at language from different times in history, use the word *era* to refer to the historic periods you are discussing. Use of the word can then be transferred to lessons with a historical focus.
- **Play a game:** 'Guess the era' where images of artefacts, people, buildings, forms of transport and so on are displayed on the interactive whiteboard for children to suggest which era they come from, giving reasons for their choice.

Linked section:
Old and new words,
page 43

Nonsense

- **Word definition:** A noun that means something that has no sense or meaning.
- **Word origin:** It seems to have originated in France, *non* meaning *no* added to *sense*, hence, 'making no sense'.
- **Word family:** Adjective: *nonsensical*.
- **Alternative words:** Balderdash, gibberish, palaver.
- **Fascinating facts:** 'The colourless green ideas sleep furiously' (Noam Chomsky) is a grammatical sentence. However, it is nonsense as it has no meaning – it can't be both colourless and green, for example. Challenge the children to invent sentences which are nonsense, pointing out that Chomsky used the form: adjective, adjective, noun, verb, adverb.
- **Activities:** Encourage the children to learn by heart verses from Lear's 'The Owl and the Pussycat' or Carroll's 'Jabberwocky'. Alternatively, they could create their own 2D or 3D versions of things mentioned in the poems – no-one can say they are wrong!

Linked section:
Nonsense words,
page 47

Fun with words

· ·

The games and activities suggested here should certainly stimulate the children's interest and curiosity about how words originated and how we use them. Once learned in school, they can take the ideas home to play with families and bring back any interesting outcomes to share in school.

Super countdown
● How many words can children come up with in a limited time that could have the prefix 'super-' added? Can they also explain what the words would mean?

Dead words
● Ask the children to list words used today that they think may die out in the future. Can they explain why?

Word wall
● Build a 'working wall' ongoing display where the children bring in examples they have found of any of the types of words they have been working on. Have sections for nonsense words, new and old words and so on.

Word play
● Some businesses use language in unusual and interesting ways to create their names, for example, by combining words, using puns or playing around with spellings. Hairdressers are often good examples of this. How many can the children find or invent?

Foreign languages
● Challenge the children to see how many words they can find that have their origins in the modern foreign language your school has chosen to teach.

Maxi, mini, micro
● Play with the language of size, by asking the children to see what examples they can find of words using these prefixes. Display the words appropriately, in sequential order.

Dictionary definitions
● As a quick starter activity, provide a word that the children are unlikely to know together with three possible definitions, one of which is the real one. Label them 'a', 'b', and 'c'. When you have read them out a couple of times, ask the children to show you on individual whiteboards which of the definitions they think is the most likely. Ask individuals to give reasons for their choices.

Guess the word
● Tell the children you are thinking of a word and they have to work out what it is. They can ask questions such as: *Does it have a prefix/suffix? Is it a compound word? Is it from a foreign language?* Before playing for the first time, let the children work out possible useful questions.

Chapter 3

Grammar

Introduction

Because of the difference between spoken and written language children do not automatically use as broad a vocabulary as we would like in their writing. They often use the first words that come into their mind, without a great deal of thought. This chapter focuses on some of the main ingredients for helping children to improve their writing – widening their working knowledge of verbs, adverbs, adjectives and connectives, alongside their ability to match their writing to a particular audience or for a particular purpose.

Poster notes

Parts of speech (page 57)

The poster gives brief explanations of nouns, verbs, adjectives and adverbs, as well as some examples of each. Several of the nouns are capitalised because they are proper nouns, as opposed to common nouns. Children can use this for reference when they are writing. The verbs are in the past tense, so that you can use them to look at tenses as well. The adjectives have been chosen for their cross-curricular value as well as providing alternatives to more commonly used words. Categorising adverbs can be difficult, as children tend to think only of the 'ly' ending, so several other types of adverb have been included for discussion and reference.

In this chapter

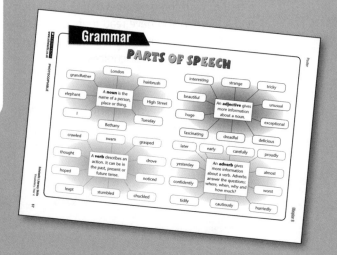

Grammar

PARTS OF SPEECH

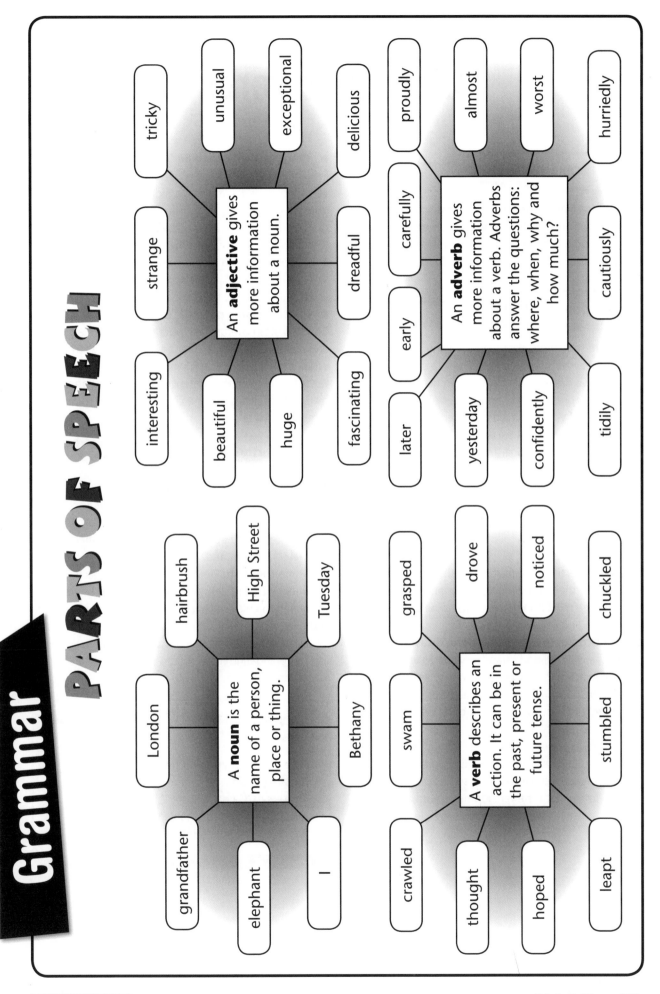

Alternative verbs

Objectives

To use alternative words that are more accurate and interesting than the most common choices. To identify and use more powerful and interesting verbs.

Background knowledge

Verbs are sometimes described as 'doing' or 'action' words. They tell us what actions people or things are doing, have done or will do. Children need to know about past, present and future tenses of verbs. A useful test of whether a word is a verb is that you can change its tense. Verbs are essential – every sentence must contain at least one. The shortest sentence possible contains two words, but one of them will be a verb, such as *Emma cried* or *He escaped*.

Activities

Through the activities in this section the children will broaden their knowledge of verbs and consider choosing the most appropriate verbs in different contexts.

● **Photocopiable page 59 'Garden disaster!'**
Ensure the children understand what verbs are, perhaps by miming actions for a variety of verbs. Not all the verbs in the passage need to be changed, so let pairs of children discuss those they feel could be changed to improve the report. The most likely choices are provided on the answer sheet (on the CD-ROM), but be prepared to accept suitable alternatives. One new verb may replace two consecutive words in some cases. Ask the children to highlight the verbs to begin with and discuss those they would change to improve the piece.

● **Photocopiable page 60 'Television documentary'**
Explain what a 'voiceover' is. Stress that this is about verbs, not adverbs, to avoid children writing *walks quickly*, *walks slowly* and so on. Tell them to avoid using the same verb twice and try to write verbs to describe the different types of movement each animal might make, for example a monkey does not just *jump*. As an extension ask the children to write their own voiceovers, using the work they have done on the sheet as a basis.

● **Photocopiable page 61 'Exploring verbs'**
Children often overuse the word *went*, so this activity draws their attention to a range of possible alternatives. While some of the missing words require fairly obvious verbs to complete the sentence, others could offer several possibilities. Tell the children to avoid using the same verb twice.

Further ideas

● **Voiceover:** Using the ideas from their television documentary sheets, ask the children to rehearse, then perform, a short voiceover for one of the animals. This could be related to appropriate video clips, where the original sound is muted.

● **Mime the verb:** Prepare a set of cards, each with a different verb written on. Choose verbs that can easily be mimed, such as *smile*, *clap*, *hop*, *frown*, *shrug*, *fidget* and *blink*. Tell a child to pick a card from the upturned pack and perform the mime for others to guess. Extend this by conjugating the verb into past, present and future tenses.

 What's on the CD-ROM

On the CD-ROM you will find:
● Printable versions of all three photocopiable pages.
● Answers to 'Garden disaster!'.
● Interactive versions of 'Garden disaster!' and 'Television documentary'.

Alternative verbs

Garden disaster!

■ Junior reporter Sam Speed's first news report needs some editing. The story's good, but Sam does not seem to know many interesting verbs. Can you suggest better ones?

■ Highlight or underline the verbs you want to change and write them in the grid below together with your suggested alternative.

The garden at Mill Lane School is in the news again! Last year it got first prize in the Our Town in Bloom competition and everyone at the school was happy. However, at the weekend something bad went on. When Mr Trent, the Head Teacher, got to school on Monday morning he saw a terrible sight. The garden had been spoiled.

"It wasn't like this on Friday night," said Mr Trent. "I think someone came in over the weekend and for some reason they spoiled our garden," he said.

Abi, a pupil at the school, said, "It makes me feel really sad. We all worked hard in the garden and now it looks terrible. All our hard work has been spoiled."

The school had worked hard to raise money to make the garden look really good. Judges in last year's competition said it had got first prize because it was well looked after and had an unusual design. Everyone at the school wants to fix the garden so they can go in for the competition again this summer.

Verbs I want to change	My suggestions

Alternative verbs

Television documentary

■ World-famous naturalist David Edinburgh has filmed a television documentary about the ways in which different animals move. With filming complete, David now has to write the voiceover. How can he keep the interest of viewers by choosing the best verbs to describe the ways the animals move?

■ In the grid, list different verbs that could be used to describe the various movements each animal might make. Make them as interesting as you can. There are some ideas to get you started.

Animal	Verbs to describe its movement
ant	scurries
monkey	
tortoise	
fish	glides
eagle	
tiger	prowls
kangaroo	
crab	
snake	
crocodile	
elephant	

Alternative verbs

Exploring verbs

■ Use a dictionary or thesaurus to help you find as many words as you can that could be used in place of the verb **went** and list them here.

■ Choose words from your list to add to the biography below.

■ It is not surprising that James became an explorer, as he has always been a very active person, with many interests. Here are just some of his adventures so far.

He _____ to Spain in a single-seat plane.

He _____ across an Australian desert on a camel.

He _____ down Swiss mountains on skis.

He _____ through mountain passes in India.

He _____ across the African plains.

He _____ to France across the Channel.

He _____ through muddy swamps in Malaysia.

He _____ through a haunted house.

He _____ to the top of Mount Everest.

He _____ into deep rainforests in Brazil.

He _____ across Texas on horseback.

Illustrations © 2010, Catherine Ward.

Adjectives and adverbs

Objectives

To identify adverbs, use them in writing and understand the impact of them. To use adjectives to improve written descriptions.

Background knowledge

Children may need reminding about the various parts of speech: that nouns are naming words and adjectives describe nouns; that verbs describe actions and that adverbs give more information about those actions: how, when or where the action happened. Use poster page 57 'Parts of speech' for this. While many adverbs end in 'ly', this is not true for all, for instance, adverbs of time such as *yesterday*, *soon* and *next*, and adverbs of place such as *inside*, *upstairs* and *between*. Adverbs answer the questions: *where*, *when*, *why*, *how* and *to what degree?*

Activities

In this section, the children will see how writing can be improved and made more informative or interesting for the reader, with the appropriate use of adjectives and adverbs.

● **Photocopiable page 63 'Pirates of the seven seas'**

Remind the children what adjectives are and what job they do: they 'add' detail or information about a noun. Remind the class about work they have done on synonyms, choosing commonly used adjectives such as *big*, *nice* or *frightened* to gather a bank of more interesting alternatives that provide more detailed information. Children do not have to deliberately choose adjectives to fit the gaps in the narrative – any will do. The final results are likely to be funny, so use this as the basis for a discussion about the importance of appropriate choices.

● **Photocopiable page 64 'Chocolate brownies'**

Remind the class that adverbs 'add' something to a verb. Ensure that the children know the meanings of the adverbs used. More confident readers could find out for themselves using a dictionary, while an adult could talk about the words with less confident readers. Let the children start with the easiest, leaving fewer choices for those they find more difficult. Ask the children who finish this activity quickly to think of some synonyms for the adverbs used to keep the sense of the recipe.

● **Photocopiable page 65 'Animal alphabet'**

The adjectives in this example all come before the noun, while the adverbs follow the verbs. They could be differently constructed, for example, the first sentence could read: *Al is an ant who is anxious and busily he flies*, a construction perhaps more suited to poetry. When the children begin to choose their own animals, the verbs they select to go with them need some thought if the following adverbs are to make sense and follow the alliterative pattern. Before starting, assign groups several letters to list interesting adverbs and adjectives for each letter. These could be written on large sheets of paper and displayed as a support for the whole class.

Further ideas

● **Adjective game:** One player says a noun and the other players have to give as many adjectives as they can to give more information about it.

● **Yum yum:** The recipe for the chocolate brownies works, so you could make them.

● **Alphabet alliteration:** Following the pattern of photocopiable page 65 'Animal alphabet', use other categories such as people's jobs or places they live, extending it by including the verb in the pattern. For example, *Amy is an amiable artist who argued animatedly; Ben is a burly builder from Birmingham who builds bungalows beautifully.*

 **What's on the CD-ROM**

On the CD-ROM you will find:
● Printable versions of all three photocopiable pages.
● Answers to 'Chocolate brownies'.
● Interactive versions of 'Pirates of the seven seas' and 'Chocolate brownies'.

Adjectives and adverbs

Pirates of the seven seas

■ Write any ten good adjectives in the grid below.

■ Use your adjectives to fill in the gaps in the story. You can make it sound as funny as you like.

Captain Jack Bluebird stood on the deck of his _____ ship, the

_____ Adventurer, and spoke to his crew. "You all know what

we are going to do. On that _____ island over there is the

_____ treasure left by my grandfather, Captain Bob Thrush.

When we find it, it will make us all _____ rich."

The _____ pirates cheered, but were soon

silenced as Captain Jack raised his hand and bellowed "Not so fast my

_____ crew! It won't be that easy. Someone else has got there

before us. Our _____ enemy, Evil Pug, is already there."

The crew gave a _____ sigh, but Jack continued

"Don't worry shipmates! We can easily beat them to the treasure! I have a

_____ plan!"

Name:

Adjectives and adverbs

Chocolate brownies

■ Use these adverbs to fill in the gaps so that the recipe makes sense.

vigorously	exactly	evenly	occasionally	gently
slowly	soon	carefully	firstly	nearly

How to make chocolate brownies
What you need:

- 50g chocolate
- 125g caster sugar
- 75g butter
- 100g self-raising flour
- 2 eggs
- Pinch of salt
- 50g chopped walnuts

What you do:

_____ put the chocolate and butter into a bowl.

_____ bring some water to the boil in a pan. (The

bowl must fit on top of the pan _____.)

With the bowl over the pan, _____ melt the chocolate

and butter, stirring _____.

Beat in the eggs and sugar _____.

_____ mix in the flour, salt and nuts.

Spread the mixture _____ in a well-greased 20cm

square tin. Bake in a moderate oven (180°C, 350°F or Gas Mark 4) for about

30 minutes until the top has a dull crust.

Now your brownies are _____ ready. This is a good

time to do the washing up.

Leave to cool and _____ you will be enjoying delicious

chocolate brownies.

Adjectives and adverbs

Animal alphabet

■ Choose interesting adjectives and adverbs to fill the gaps in this poem. Make sure your chosen words match the right letter of the alphabet! The first two lines are done for you.

Al is an **anxious** ant who runs **angrily**.

Bet is a **beautiful** butterfly who flies **busily**.

Cuddles is a _____ cat who sleeps _____

Dora is _____ dog who barks _____

Egbert is an _____ elephant who swims _____

Flo is a _____ fox who eats _____

Gordon is a _____ giraffe who strides _____

■ Continue the poem, choosing names and animals of your own.

_____

_____

_____

_____

_____

_____

_____

_____

_____

_____

_____

_____

_____

Formal and informal words

Objectives

To decide how to choose the best words for different audiences. To understand the difference between writing for formal and informal purposes.

Background knowledge

Most language that children have direct knowledge of will be informal, although they will be aware of contextual language; that we adapt our spoken language to fit in with different situations. They will also know that spoken and written language are often different, although this knowledge may not be explicit. It is helpful to explain what is meant by the words *formal* and *informal*.

Activities

This section focuses on using the appropriate language in a particular context. Take care not to undervalue children's spoken language. You should stress that we all use different forms of language for different situations and that knowing how and when to use more formal language has to be learned.

● **Photocopiable page 67 'When you meet an important person'**
This activity should get children thinking about the differences between formal and informal ways of speaking and about using language appropriate to the situation. It also provides an opportunity to reinforce the use of speech marks. Before starting the activity, have a discussion with the class about who the important person might be and why it would be polite to use more formal language.

● **Photocopiable page 68 'Invitations'**
This activity muddles up the formal and informal language of party invitations. Sort sample sets of blank invitations of different types into 'formal' and 'informal' before doing the activity so that the children begin to assimilate the different sorts of language used. They should explain how they made their choices.

● **Photocopiable page 69 'Friends online'**
This activity focuses on the very informal language used in online messaging conversations. It offers an opportunity for discussing how language is changing with modern communication methods and how using this type of language, while appropriate in this context, would be inappropriate in other situations.

Further ideas

● **Don't put your foot in it!:** List situations when formal or informal language is usually used or most appropriate.

● **The right words:** Play a game where the children have to suggest what might be an appropriate thing to say in a given situation. For example, apologising for breaking a cup or treading on someone's toe, saying thank you for a present you don't like and making up with a friend you have argued with.

● **When you meet an important person:** Use appropriate intonation to perform the poems from photocopiable page 67 'When you meet an important person'. While the poems are being read, let pairs of children mime the activities for each verse.

What's on the CD-ROM

On the CD-ROM you will find:
● Printable versions of all three photocopiable pages.
● Answers to 'Invitations'.
● Interactive version of 'Invitations'.

When you meet an important person

■ When you meet an important person, there are all sorts of rules you must follow, including the way you speak. Complete the rhyme to help you remember what to say so you will be well prepared. The first verse is done for you.

When you meet an important person
Please keep this in your head
Don't say **"Hi"** to that person,
Say **"Good morning"** instead.

When you meet an important person

Please keep this in your head

Don't say _____ to that person,

Say _____ instead.

When you meet an important person

Please keep this in your head

Don't say _____ to that person,

Say _____ instead.

When you meet an important person

Please keep this in your head

Don't say _____ to that person,

Say _____ instead.

When you meet an important person

Please keep this in your head

Don't say _____ to that person,

Say _____ instead.

Name:

Invitations

■ Two birthday invitations have got muddled up. Cut out the sentences below. Sort them into an invitation for an adult's party and an invitation for a child's party. The clues are in the kind of language that is used. Write the new invitations on another sheet of paper. (There are seven sentences in each invitation.)

Refreshments will be provided.
It's all happening at my house.
Dress casually.
RSVP
Wear your jeans and t-shirt.
Time: 3pm – 6pm
Let me know if you can come!
The venue is my home.
I really hope you'll be there.
You are invited to attend a party to celebrate my birthday.
There'll be lots of yummy food.
It's my birthday! Can you come to my party?
It starts at 3 o'clock and will end at 6 o'clock.
I do hope you are able to attend.

Formal and informal words

Friends online

■ Tobi and Anya are helping to organise a stall at the school fête. They are sharing their ideas using their favourite online messenger site. What else might they say to each other about their ideas and plans?

Tobi: Hiya

Anya: Hiya

Tobi: Watcha got then?

Anya: Loadsa stuff!!!!

Tallest Sunflower Competition

Tobi: Yeah but is any of it any good?

Anya: Course! Wanna know my best idea?

Tobi: Course! What is it then?

Anya: People pay 50p for a sunflower seed and a pot for a grow-the-tallest-sunflower competition. Whaddya think?

Tobi: _____

_____

_____

_____

_____

_____

_____

_____

_____

_____

_____

Illustrations © 2010, Catherine Ward.

Connectives

Objective

To use connectives to create compound sentences.

Background knowledge

The most common connectives that children use are *and*, *but*, *because* and *then*. Making the children conscious of a wider variety of these important function words lifts their writing to a new level. When we talk about connectives with Year 4 children, we usually mean words or phrases that connect two or more sentences together, changing a simple sentence with one verb to a compound sentence with more than one verb. The types of connectives known as 'conjunctions', such as *but*, *when* and *because*, and those known as 'connecting adverbs', such as *however*, function differently. Conjunctions join clauses within a sentence. Connecting adverbs connect ideas but the clauses remain separate sentences.

Activities

In these activities the children will explore the use of connectives that signal time, those that offer alternatives, those that provide additions and those that are linked to cause and effect.

● **Photocopiable page 71 'Lifecycle of the butterfly'**
This explanation text uses connectives to begin some sentences, to make children aware that they can be used in this way. Some of the connectives may be used more than once, although try to discourage them from overusing *because*. However, you may be prepared to accept this from less confident writers. Challenge more confident writers to look for examples where they can suggest more than one suitable alternative.

● **Photocopiable page 72 'Good news, bad news'**
This activity asks the children to choose suitable words to replace the connective *but*. There are more suggestions in the word bank than are needed, to allow children to consider appropriate choices.

● **Photocopiable page 73 'Time connectives'**
In this activity the children are required to use alternatives to the connective *then*, which is linked to time and much overused by children in both their speaking and writing. The oral activity that precedes the writing will help to reinforce alternative choices and make them realise just how much they rely on the word *then*. As a starter, choose settings such as the beach or events such as a party, for small groups to describe an activity without using the word *then*. If they say *then*, the person who spots it carries on.

Further ideas

● **Cross-curricular:** Connectives are generic function words and as such can be used across the curriculum. Providing opportunities to use them in subject areas other than literacy will help reinforcement and automaticity.

● **Working wall:** Challenge the class to find as many connectives as possible under the headings 'Then', 'But', 'And' and 'Because', to develop your own list of words to be used in place of these most common connectives.

● **Thought for the day:** Choose a theme, such as dinosaurs, food, friendship or anything else that's relevant to the children's experiences. Give out sets of laminated cards, with different connectives, to groups of children. Let them take turns to turn over a card and use it to say something about the theme.

What's on the CD-ROM

On the CD-ROM you will find:
● Printable versions of all three photocopiable pages.
● Answers to 'Lifecycle of the butterfly'.
● Interactive version of 'Lifecycle of the butterfly'.

Connectives

Lifecycle of the butterfly

■ Choose suitable connectives to fill in the gaps.

Connectives about time	Connectives about causes and effects	Connectives that offer alternatives
when once as until	because so consequently	although however

The lifecycle of the butterfly

It all begins in early summer _____ a female butterfly

lays her eggs. _____ the mother butterfly does not

stay to look after the eggs, she has laid them in places that are hard to see,

_____ they are fairly safe. _____ the

eggs grow, tiny caterpillars develop inside them. _____

their mother has chosen the right kind of plant, the newly hatched

caterpillars have food straight away, _____ they grow

quickly. _____, life for caterpillars can be dangerous,

_____ they may be eaten by insects or birds. They keep eating

_____ it is time for the next stage _____

they must find a suitable place to make themselves a cocoon. Inside the cocoon,

another change is taking place _____ the caterpillar is

transforming into a butterfly. _____ the butterfly finally

emerges, the lifecycle is ready to begin all over again.

Name:

Connectives

Good news, bad news

■ Write notes for the script for tonight's news so that the newsreaders each have one good and one bad news story. Use the topics and decide what the story should be. You could write the full script on another sheet of paper.

■ There is an example to help you get started. Begin each piece of good news with a connective that can replace the word **but** from the list below.

Connectives to use in place of **but** to start your story		
alternatively although despite whereas except besides yet nevertheless on the other hand		

News topic	Bad news	Good news
Farming	Unfortunately, the recent heavy rain could spoil the wheat harvest this year.	However, the damp conditions mean that thousands of frogs are eating the slugs that destroy many crops.
Sport		
Fashion		
Pets		
Weather		
TV		

Connectives

Time connectives

■ Choose any game from this list with your partner.

tennis   football   rounders   rugby   netball   hockey

■ Take turns to explain how to play the game, using time connectives from this grid. (You will probably use each word at the beginning of your sentence.)

before	next	after	soon
first	finally	after that	later
meanwhile	until	when	while

■ Carry on until you have explained how it works. Then choose another game.
■ After talking about two or three different games, choose one to write an explanation for. Remember to use the time connectives to make your explanation interesting.

How to play _____

_____

_____

_____

_____

_____

_____

_____

Assessment

Assessment grid

The following grid shows the main objectives and activities covered in this chapter. You can use the grid to locate activities that cover a particular focus that you are keen to monitor.

Objective	Page	Activity title
To use alternative words that are more accurate and interesting than the most common choices.	59 60 61	Garden disaster! Television documentary Exploring verbs
To identify and use more powerful and interesting verbs.	59 60 61	Garden disaster! Television documentary Exploring verbs
To identify adverbs, use them in writing and understand the impact of them.	64 65	Chocolate brownies Animal alphabet
To use adjectives to improve written descriptions.	63 65	Pirates of the seven seas Animal alphabet
To decide how to choose the best words for different audiences.	67 68 69	When you meet an important person Invitations Friends online
To understand the difference between writing for formal and informal purposes.	67 68 69	When you meet an important person Invitations Friends online
To use connectives to create compound sentences.	71 72 73	Lifecycle of the butterfly Good news, bad news Time connectives

Observation and record keeping

Use some of the objectives from each section outside literacy lessons. Encourage the children to use what they have learned as success criteria in other contexts, so that you can record their progress in each area. Note those children who can transfer their learning and those who find this difficult.

Assessment activity

● **What you need**
Photocopiable page 75 'Roll up! Roll up!'.
● **What to do**
Gather information from the class about circus acts. Let the children mime the circus acts mentioned on the photocopiable sheet to help them think of appropriate words to use. Remind the class about persuasive language and the necessity of using words economically on a poster that people spend only a short time reading.

Differentiation

● Ask the less confident writers in the class to write just a verb and adverb for each category, or let an adult scribe their chosen words next to a picture they have drawn in each of the spaces on the sheet.
● Encourage more confident writers to select one of the categories to write about in greater detail.

Further learning

● **Guided reading:** Ask groups to look for particular parts of speech when working in guided reading, to record in a bank of useful verbs, adjectives and adverbs.
● **Writing success criteria:** Encourage the children to suggest success criteria for pieces of writing, where particular word use is significant, for example, 'Use at least three adverbs' in a poem.
● **Comparing language:** Can the children point out the differences in how language is used in contrasting television programmes, such as the news and a soap opera.

Assessment

Roll up! Roll up!

■ Circus Rinaldi wants as many people as possible to come to its show. Choose the best adjectives, verbs and adverbs and use them to write captions on the poster.

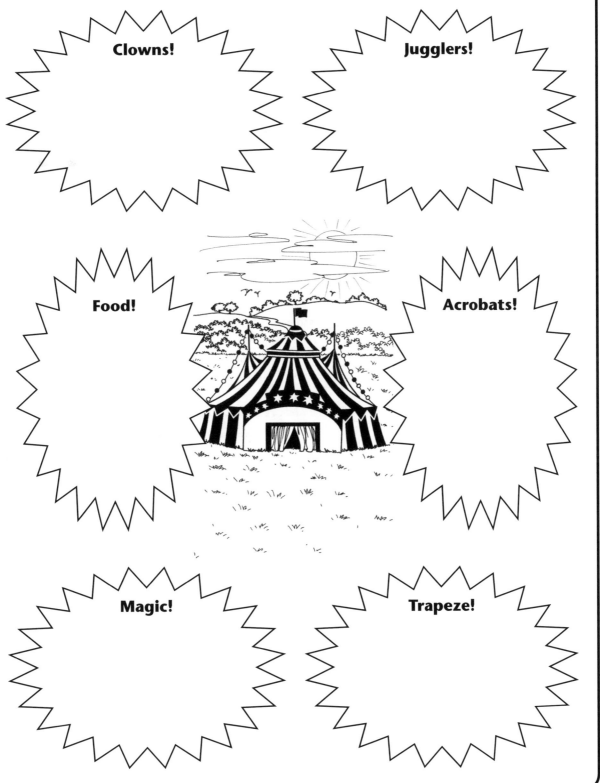

Clowns!

Jugglers!

Food!

Acrobats!

Magic!

Trapeze!

Illustrations © 2010, Catherine Ward.

Word of the week

The Word of the week pages provide information on one word linked to each section in the chapter. Each word is described in some of the following categories: word definition, word origin, word family, alternative words, fascinating facts and activities. Not all categories are relevant to every word.

You can use the words as a focus to support your work on the different sections of the chapter. For example, you could create a display around it. The information is a starting point for a word focus. The words could form part of your classroom living word bank.

You could also use the word of the week as a springboard to inspire children to think about or research fascinating facts about words, find interesting quotations and to encourage them to use dictionaries and thesauruses.

Agreed

- **Word definition:** A verb meaning to be alike in opinion.
- **Word origin:** From French *agréer* meaning to accept or to receive kindly.
- **Word family:** Verb: *agree*; noun: *agreement*.
- **Alternative words:** Accept, consent, concur, acknowledge.
- **Fascinating facts:** A gentleman's agreement is an informal agreement between two people and is based on the honour of completing a deal rather than a legal requirement.
- **Activities:** Let the children role play disagreements in PSHE using drama to explain how they finally agreed on a resolution to the problem. After a class debate, ask the children to vote on the proposition being debated. Announce and display the total who agreed or disagreed.

Linked section:
Alternative verbs,
page 58

Carefully

- **Word definition:** An adverb meaning to take care or be cautious.
- **Word family:** Verb and noun: *care*; noun: *carer*.
- **Alternative words:** Attentively, delicately, thoughtfully.
- **Fascinating facts:** The Hawaiian name *Akahele*, for a boy or girl, and the Hebrew name *Zehira* both mean careful or cautious.
- **Activities:** Tell the children to collate a list of things that must be done carefully, in relation to health and safety in different situations, for example, crossing the road, cooking or using electrical apparatus. Write poems based on the idea that parents are always telling children to 'be careful'. The first line of each verse could be *Mum told me to be careful*, with the final line *and so I did it carefully*, or *but I didn't do it carefully*.

Linked section:
Adjectives and
adverbs, page 62

Context

- **Word definition:** A noun meaning the place in which something belongs or the background of an event.
- **Word origin:** From the Latin *contextus* which means to join together.
- **Word family:** Verb: *contextualise.*
- **Alternative words:** Background, relation, situation.
- **Fascinating facts:** An archaeological context is an event in time which has been preserved. It includes the place, the type of soil and so on.
- **Activities:** Use it when working on settings in reading or writing, as the setting can provide the context for the narrative. To make concrete the abstract idea of context, ask the children to draw a person dressed both correctly and incorrectly for a particular type of weather.

> **Linked section:**
> Formal and informal words, page 66

Although

- **Word definition:** A co-ordinating conjunction that joins two clauses of equal weight, which can also be used at the start of a sentence. Watch out for misspellings using double 'l' and adding an 'r' where children have confused though with through. It means in spite of or but.
- **Word origin:** From Middle English *al thogh.*
- **Word family:** Conjunction: *though.*
- **Alternative words:** But, whereas, despite, though.
- **Fascinating facts:** 'Although nature commences with reason and ends in experience it is necessary for us to do the opposite, that is to commence with experience and from this to proceed to investigate the reason.' Leonardo da Vinci.
- **Activities:** Play 'The glad game' from the story *Pollyanna*, where something that appears to be disappointing is turned into something positive. Let the children take turns to begin a sentence with although, such as *Although she had to stay in bed with a bad cold…*, which their partner might complete with: *…she was glad to have the time to read her comics.*

> **Linked section:**
> Connectives, page 70

Fun with words

· ·

Here are some suggestions for quick starter games or ongoing visual activities to reinforce the types of language covered in this chapter.

My Granny went shopping
● Play the game where each child must use an appropriate adjective to describe what Granny bought. Extend this to make the adjectives alliterative. Have a round where each child must think of two adjectives. To help the children to realise that it is possible to overload writing with adjectives, have a game where the class try to list as many adjectives as possible for the items in Granny's shopping basket, so that it quickly begins to sound ridiculous.

Today I'm feeling…
● Play the game where you provide an adjective describing a feeling or emotion, such as *happy*, *sad* or *excited*, and the children have to list as many alternatives as they can.

More good news
● Extend the idea of photocopiable page 72 'Good news, bad news' by displaying a piece of (fictional) bad news on the wall, inviting the children to add their 'good news' comments underneath, with a suitable connective.

Message boards
● Have fun with an on-the-wall messaging board, a version of online messaging, where you provide a starter statement or question and the children can add their informally written comments.

Character links
● The children can create a bank of statements that describe a wide range of characters, with short but interesting descriptive phrases such as …*was extremely happy*; …*ate their meal ravenously*; …*tiptoed gently across the hallway*, and so on. Make these into a pack of laminated cards, which is placed face down between a group of players, who take turns to turn over the top two cards. They must use any suitable connective to link the two sentences together, choosing their own pronoun – *he*, *she*, *we*, *I* or *they*. The results are likely to be very funny.

Cross-curricular vocabulary

Introduction

In the primary school, we are in the fortunate position of being able to find opportunities to transfer learning between and across subjects, so that in this case, vocabulary learned within the context of literacy can be used in other subject areas. Teaching such 'technical' vocabulary will help children to develop a sound conceptual understanding of essential elements of the subjects and fulfil the requirements of the National Curriculum, where specific vocabulary is useful for cross-curricular work.

In this chapter

Geography page 81	To use vocabulary relating to settlement, the environment and mapping.
History page 85	To use vocabulary relating to the passage of time, aspects of society, and fact and opinion.
Mathematics page 89	To use vocabulary relating to the four operations, shape and handling data.
Science page 93	To use vocabulary relating to the explanation of scientific processes.
Assessment page 97	Activities and ideas to assess the understanding of specific technical vocabulary in geography, history, mathematics and science.

Poster notes

Classifying connectives (page 80)
Having a working knowledge of connectives that serve particular purposes will help the children to organise their non-fiction writing. So much subject-based writing is explanatory in nature and the way in which the connectives are grouped on the poster will help the children across the curriculum. For example, when writing a chronological report or a set of instructions, direct the children to the sequencing connectives. Discussion texts can use the contrasting connectives while explanations might use the illustrating connectives, and so on.

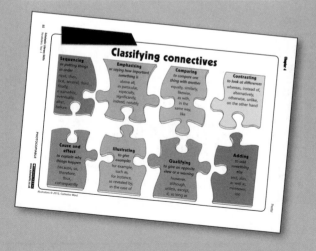

Cross-curricular vocabulary

Classifying connectives

Contrasting
to look at differences

whereas, instead of,
alternatively,
otherwise, unlike,
on the other hand

Adding
to add
something
else

and, also,
as well as,
moreover,
too

Comparing
to compare one
thing with another

equally, similarly,
likewise,
as with,
in the
same way,
like

Qualifying
to give an opposite
view or a warning

however,
although,
unless, except,
if, as long as

Emphasising
or saying how important
something is

above all,
in particular,
especially,
significantly,
indeed, notably

Illustrating
to give
examples

for example,
such as,
for instance,
as revealed by,
in the case of

Sequencing
or putting things
in order

next, then,
first, second, third...
finally,
meanwhile,
eventually,
after,
before

**Cause and
effect**
to explain why
things happen

because, so,
therefore,
thus,
consequently

Illustrations © 2010, Catherine Ward.

PHOTOCOPIABLE   **SCHOLASTIC**
www.scholastic.co.uk

Geography

Objective

To use vocabulary relating to settlement, the environment and mapping.

Background knowledge

Rather than choosing vocabulary that is specific to particular units of work, the language in this section is more generic, so that it can be used across many aspects of geographical study. The more the children are able to use subject-specific vocabulary, the more they will develop their knowledge and conceptual understanding of what the words represent. Many of the words are abstract, which will be a big jump in understanding for some children.

Activities

The activities in this section focus on vocabulary associated with the geographical themes of settlement, the environment and maps, areas that can occur within a range of topics.

● **Photocopiable page 82 'How settlements developed'**
There are some challenging words and concepts in this activity, which more confident learners will enjoy, but less confident learners will need some guidance with. Before starting the written activity, ask groups of children to stand physically close to each other, so that they are 'in close proximity', making either a 'nucleated' or a 'linear' shape. This will help them develop a better understanding of the new vocabulary.

● **Photocopiable page 83 'The changing environment'**
Although the context for this activity is global warming, the vocabulary is relevant to many aspects of the environment, particularly the words *weather, climate, urban, rural* and *impact*. Have a class debate on the subject either before or after the children complete the photocopiable sheet.

● **Photocopiable page 84 'Mapping the way'**
Because this activity is based on a story narrative, it should help the children to realise that understanding how maps work is not a discrete activity. As well as a vital element of geographical study, it is also a life skill.

Further ideas

● **Settlement search:** Use local maps to find examples of linear and nucleated settlements.
● **Orienteering:** Set up a basic orienteering course in the school grounds where teams of children follow clues and use a map of the area to find objects. Remind the children to use appropriate vocabulary.

 What's on the CD-ROM

On the CD-ROM you will find:
● Printable versions of all three photocopiable pages.
● Answers to 'How settlements developed' and 'Mapping the way'.
● Interactive versions of 'How settlements developed' and 'Mapping the way'.

Name:

Geography

How settlements developed

■ Use the words below to fill in the gaps in this magazine article.

landscape	physical	communities	hamlet	city
resources	villages	features	agriculture	linear	remote
nucleated	valley	proximity	necessities

Have you ever wondered how settlements came to be where they are? It

didn't just happen by chance. From the smallest _____ to

the largest _____ there are particular _____ of

the _____ that helped people choose them as places to live.

_____ characteristics such as having a source of water nearby,

some natural shelter from trees or higher ground and good flat land for

_____ were important. Such things were the _____

for sustaining life.

　　However, it's hard to live on a mountain! So often settlements grew up lower

down, in a _____. Sometimes _____ were very

_____, with the nearest neighbours living many miles away – a

long way to travel on foot. However, in some places, many settlements grew in

close _____ to each other, with everyone making the most of the

natural _____ around them. Some of these places grew out from

the centre. We call this type a _____ settlement, whereas others

developed along a route or a river making long, stretched out shapes, called a

_____ settlement. Over time, many small _____

joined together to form towns. Maybe you live in one of them!

Geography

The changing environment

■ What is best for the environment? We can't always agree.
■ Use the words below to write a discussion between two people who have different views. One thinks we need to make changes and one thinks we are already doing enough. The conversation has been started for you.

conversation	weather	climate	rural	recycling	impact
pollution	conserve	sustain	urban		

Mrs Tooky: We have to act now to stop the dreadful pollution that is destroying our planet.

Mr Gregor: But we are doing fine! We already have a huge recycling programme.

Mrs Tooky: _____

_____

_____

Mr Gregor: _____

_____

_____

Mrs Tooky: _____

_____

_____

Mr Gregor: _____

_____

_____

Name:

Geography

Mapping the way

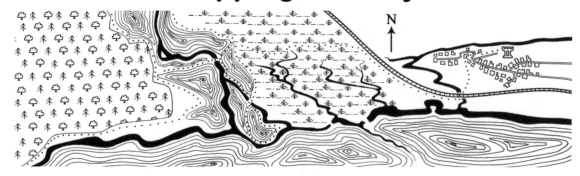

■ Complete the story using words from the box below.

> route   scale   distance   direction   key   symbol
> network   grid reference   compass   journey
> itinerary   kilometres   population

Jai crept slowly out of the wood, no longer protected by its dense cover. Which

way to go? He took out the map the boss had given him. Which _____

should he take? He lay his _____ on the map and soon found north.

With a river, a gorge and a swamp to get through this would not be an easy

_____. He did not know what dangers lay ahead, he only knew that

if he did not find the secret code, the mystery would not be solved. He had

been given a _____ for his destination – a village with a very small

_____ so it was easy to find especially as it had the _____

for a castle, which he double-checked with the _____ to be sure that

he was right. Mistakes now could be fatal! He calculated the _____ to

his destination as about 30 _____ and used the map to plot the best

_____. There was a complicated _____ of paths and tracks

through the swamp and Jai hoped he'd chosen well. His _____ took

him across a railway line, through a small hamlet and on a narrow track at the base

of the gorge. Thankfully this was a large _____ map so he'd managed

to find a bridge over the river. As long as it was still there, maybe he'd be OK.

PHOTOCOPIABLE   **SCHOLASTIC**
www.scholastic.co.uk

History

Objective

To use vocabulary relating to the passage of time, aspects of society, and fact and opinion.

Background knowledge

There are key concepts underlying history in the National Curriculum, which permeate the subject at all levels. Three of these form the focus for this section: *time*, *aspects of society* and *explanations*, which include fact-and-opinion and cause-and-effect. It is important that children do not learn history as a series of dates, events and undisputed facts. The right vocabulary equips them to ask questions and understand the answers, as well as realising how culture and society impacts on people and events.

Activities

There are likely to be new and perhaps difficult words for the children to learn and understand in each activity. Encourage them to use dictionaries to find definitions for this new vocabulary. When completing cloze procedure activities, using context clues or making educated guesses are valid strategies, which can involve the children in paired speaking and listening activities.

● **Photocopiable page 86 'Language origins'**
This activity can be used in conjunction with Chapter 2, where we looked at word origins in more detail. It also provides a link with work on synonyms. The language of explanation is an important element when considering historical events and actions.

● **Photocopiable page 87 'Family history autobiography'**
This topical subject provides an opportunity to use the language of time in a familiar context. *Chronological* is probably the most difficult word here, but an important addition to the children's historical vocabulary. Link it to *alphabetical* and *numerical* to help them understand it. It derives from *chrono*, the Greek for *time*.

● **Photocopiable page 88 'Advice to time travellers'**
This activity asks the children to use the vocabulary associated with aspects of society that can be used with any historical study of people in a given time period, as areas such as architecture, beliefs and technology are relevant to all societies. The words *culture*, *primitive* and *civilised* are likely to be the most difficult concepts for the children to understand, so may need prior discussion in relation to a historic period the children are familiar with.

Further ideas

● **Family trees:** Build the family tree of a well-known historical figure, relevant to your current area of study, adding comments that make use of specific vocabulary from the activity.

● **Timely advice:** Produce a class book or digital presentation of specific advice for travellers going to particular historic periods, to tie in with your current focus or theme.

 **What's on the CD-ROM**

On the CD-ROM you will find:
● Printable versions of all three photocopiable pages.
● Answers to 'Language origins' and 'Family history autobiography'.
● Interactive versions of 'Language origins' and 'Family history autobiography'.

History

Language origins

■ Use words from the box to fill in the gaps in the explanation below.

because   reason   view   result   effect   outcome
caused   fact   opinion   explain   consequence   origins

Have you ever wondered where our language came from? There is more

than one _____ to _____ why we

have the words we use every day. It's a _____ that most

English words have their _____ in another language. This

has happened _____ Great Britain not only had tribes of

its own long ago, but has also been invaded several times in the past. One

_____ of these invasions was the _____

they had on our language. As a _____ we have many words

from French, Latin, Greek and Norse. This doesn't mean that we can all speak

those languages! The words have changed from the originals over the years,

but one _____ of this is that we do already know quite

a bit of other languages, even though we may not realise it! This mixture has

_____ us to have a quite

complicated language. In some people's

_____ this is one of the

reasons why many English words can be difficult

to spell. Whatever your _____

it is hard to deny that English spelling can be very

strange at times.

History

Family history autobiography

■ Daniel has been researching his family history and has begun writing an autobiography. Use words from the box to complete it.

recent	distant	ancient	modern	decade	records	antique
century	ancestor	chronological	period	generations		

I have decided to begin this autobiography by going as far back as I can

to my most _____ _____. I have looked at

_____ going back over several _____ and have

discovered that my great-great-grandfather was a seaman called Thomas Cooper,

who lived in the 19th _____. During this _____ of

history, he would probably have worked on a sailing ship, not that different from

those ships of the _____ world, although they may have had some

_____ equipment to make things easier for them on long voyages.

I have seen an _____ compass in a museum that may have been

like the one on Thomas's ship. I have found out about Thomas's son, my

great-grandfather James, and his son my grandfather William, and I have started to

keep a _____ list of everyone on my family tree, so that I have them

in the right order. My most _____

find was my great-great-aunt Sophie who was born

sometime in the _____ of the 1920s,

so I'm looking forward to learning more about her as

I carry on with my research.

Illustrations © 2010, Catherine Ward.

Name:

History

Advice to time travellers

■ Write a guide of useful advice for the 'Time travellers' website. You must include the words in the box below. The guide has been started for you.

| architecture | beliefs | science | technology | culture |
| civilised | diet | agriculture | primitive | transport |

When travelling back in time, there are some important things to bear in mind. Make a note of these to ensure a successful trip:

1. People in the past will have been used to a different culture to ours. Please respect it.

2. _____

_____

_____

3. _____

_____

_____

4. _____

_____

_____

5. _____

_____

_____

6. _____

_____

_____

Mathematics

Objective

To use vocabulary relating to the four operations, shape and handling data.

Background knowledge

Knowing the correct technical vocabulary for mathematics is vital, both to understand the mathematics and when children are asked to give explanations of work they have done. Much mathematical vocabulary comes under the heading of 'metalanguage', the words we use to describe or talk about the symbols and technicalities of the subject, so that if, for example, children do not know the symbol for *greater than* they are at a disadvantage. Children also need to know that some words take on a different meaning when used in a mathematical context.

Activities

These activities focus on key vocabulary used in the areas of number and calculations, shape and handling data, and assume that the children already know and understand the simpler mathematical language.

● **Photocopiable page 90 'Ballad of the builder'**
This activity uses language associated with counting, partitioning and calculating, with a focus on the words used for explanation and sequencing.

● **Photocopiable page 91 'Shapes in the news'**
This news report links shapes with art. Some input may be needed on the words *polygon* and *vertices*, so revising the properties of shapes would fit in well with this activity. Describing 3D shapes that are felt inside a 'feely bag' for others to guess necessitates using accurate language.

● **Photocopiable page 92 'Explaining data handling'**
This activity requires the children to explain the language of data handling, using words such as *criteria*, *represent* and *interpret*, which, because they are abstract concepts, may be difficult for some Year 4 children to grasp at first. The children could look the words up in a thesaurus to find synonyms that would help to clarify the meanings for them. You may want to enlarge the photocopiable sheet to increase the space for the children to write captions.

Further ideas

● **Arty shapes:** Look at the work of artists such as Paul Klee, Georges Braque and Piet Mondrian who used geometric patterns in their paintings. Children could create their own paintings or collages based on shapes. They can then describe them using appropriate vocabulary.
● **Pictograms:** Children could make their own tally charts and pictograms based on visual stimuli, such as those used on photocopiable page 92 'Explaining data handling'.

 **What's on the CD-ROM**

On the CD-ROM you will find:
● Printable versions of all three photocopiable pages.
● Answers to 'Ballad of the builder' and 'Shapes in the news'.
● Interactive versions of 'Ballad of the builder' and 'Explaining data handling'.

Name:

Mathematics

Ballad of the builder

■ Choose words from the box to complete the builder's ballad.

| problem | solution | estimated | calculation | equation | rule |
| estimate | method | explain | prediction | reason | order |

Now Sam the builder had a plan

To build the best house in the land

But the _____ was he didn't know

How to _____ to Mr Joe

Mr Joe, the boss, had a golden _____

And Sam was certainly not a fool,

He _____ the total price

And followed Mr Joe's advice.

But the _____ was way too high

And Mr Joe gave a great big sigh.

The _____ Sam had used was wrong

So his _____ was not strong.

Sam had no _____ for his mistake

The problem made his poor head ache.

The _____ came from Mr Joe

He'd seen it on a TV show!

Sam had used the wrong _____

When he made his _____

The _____ was the wrong way round.

Sam's happy now the answer's found!

PHOTOCOPIABLE

Mathematics

Shapes in the news

■ Use words from the box below to complete the news article.

symmetrical	relationship	sort	classified	properties
vertices	polygons	irregular	construct	regular

An amazing piece of artwork has gone on display at the town art gallery this week. Made from hundreds of 3D shapes in many different colours, the work, entitled _Shapes of the future_ is by artist Layla Hammond.

We asked her about the work. "Well, it is _____ with one half reflecting the other," she told us. "I had to _____ it very carefully. I had to _____ all the shapes according to their _____, to make sure I could fit them together in the ways I wanted."

We asked how she decided which shapes to use. "I wanted to use both _____ and _____ shapes," Layla explained, "so you will see shapes you recognise and some that you can't put a name to easily. I wanted to show how they differed, but also to show the _____ between them, such as how they might fit together in different ways."

When asked how she _____ the shapes, she said that as each of the _____ had different faces and different _____, she used those to guide her. The finished piece is certainly interesting. It will be on show until the end of next week.

Explaining data handling

■ Use words from the box to help you write captions in the spaces to explain the illustrations of things you will use in data handling. Draw lines from each caption to the part of the illustration you are explaining.

represent	interpret	data	information	tally
survey	chart	criteria	collect	pictogram

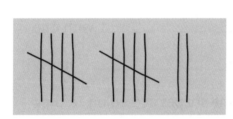

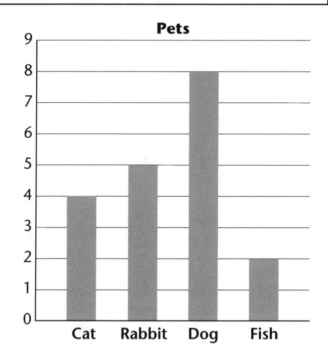

Pets

Weather August 2009

Sunny   Rainy   Sunny Spells   Cloudy

PHOTOCOPIABLE

■ SCHOLASTIC
www.scholastic.co.uk

Science

Objective

To use vocabulary relating to the explanation of scientific processes.

Background knowledge

The study of science is essentially about asking questions, posing problems and explaining findings, but children can often become so involved in the practical aspects of the subject that they may forget their original purpose or which question they were trying to answer. Having achieved a result, they can then find it difficult to explain the processes they went through to arrive there, to summarise their findings or suggest a hypothesis. This section focuses on the generic language of science that will enable them to be better acquainted with this question and answer process.

Activities

These activities use generic scientific vocabulary in a variety of situations. They are focused on the language of discovery, experimentation and explanation rather than being specific to particular content.

● **Photocopiable page 94 'Wow – the car for me!'** Most children will be familiar with the persuasive language of adverts and may be surprised to discover how much vocabulary of a scientific nature is used in them. Talk about how manufacturers use science to test and prove their products and look at examples of how advertisers use what might be called 'pseudo-science' to impress us so that we will be interested and perhaps want to buy.

● **Photocopiable page 95 'Food survey'** The questionnaire format of this activity can be used as a model for how data can be collected to answer questions, and so links with maths as well as science. Encourage the children to use this vocabulary when they talk about their own scientific investigations.

● **Photocopiable page 96 'Growing geraniums'** The vocabulary used in this report of a science investigation demonstrates how to use the language needed to convey basic information in a simple, straightforward way. Children may be unfamiliar with the word *systematic*, which can be explained by describing how systems have to work in a particular order for things to go properly, such as a central heating system.

Further ideas

● **Science adverts:** The children can search through magazines and newspapers to find examples of where science has been used as a persuasive tool, such as in beauty and household products for example.

● **Food survey:** Carry out the survey, or an adapted version of it, in the class or across the school. Ask the children to collate and interpret the results, perhaps passing them on to the school kitchen or head teacher.

● **Plant study:** Set up your own plant growth experiment. Bean seeds grow quickly, while geraniums need to be grown from cuttings.

What's on the CD-ROM

On the CD-ROM you will find:
● Printable versions of all three photocopiable pages.
● Answers to 'Wow – the car for me!' and 'Growing geraniums'.
● Interactive versions of 'Wow – the car for me!' and 'Growing geraniums'.

Name:

Science

Wow – the car for me!

■ Complete this advertisement using the words in the box.

comparison	results	evidence	proves
discover	tests	equipment	measured
demonstrate	components	observations	
conclusion	similar		

Do YOU want the best car in the street?

Of course you do! And we have just the car for you. The all-new Wow is

scientifically proven to be better than the rest. How do we know? Well…

Our engineers ran thousands of _____ to make sure everything

worked perfectly. All the _____ were excellent.

We made careful _____ of the Wow's performance in all driving

conditions and our _____ _____ it outperforms

others in its field.

We use only the best _____ in our engines.

We _____ the Wow's performance against _____

cars and can _____ its superiority.

The Wow has all the latest _____ to make your drive easy and

comfortable.

_____ the Wow for yourself. Take a test drive today and you will

come to the _____ that the Wow has no _____!

PHOTOCOPIABLE   ■SCHOLASTIC
www.scholastic.co.uk

Science

Food survey

■ Can you help Oak Tree School to find out how it can improve its school dinners? You need to think of some questions, using the words in the box that will give them useful information about people's opinions. The first two have been done for you.

| organise | improvements | fair | select | suitable |
| describe | experiment | differences | samples | suggest |

1. Do you think the food at school is **suitable** for everyone?

2. Would you **describe** school dinners as being good value?

3. _____

_____

4. _____

_____

5. _____

_____

6. _____

_____

7. _____

_____

8. _____

_____

9. _____

_____

10. _____

_____

Name:

Science

Growing geraniums

■ Class 4 carried out an experiment to discover the best way to grow geraniums to plant in their school garden. Here is the report of what they did. Fill in the gaps with words from the box.

| record | monitor | effect | outcome | systematic |
| observations | predicted | evaluation | diagram | investigate |

We wanted to _____ how plants grow, so first we drew a

_____ to show what we planned to do. After that we put the

plants in different places. Some had light, some had no light; some were given

water and some had no water. We wanted to see what _____ the

different conditions would have. We also made a chart so that we could keep a

_____ of how the plants were doing. We all _____

what we thought would happen to each plant.

   Next we set up a rota of people whose job it was to _____ and

check the plants each day. Because we wanted to be very _____, we

checked them at the same time every day, and wrote down our

_____. After two weeks we did

an _____ to see which plants had

been given the best growing conditions. The

_____ of our experiment was

that plants need light, warmth and water to

grow well.

Illustrations © 2010, Catherine Ward.

PHOTOCOPIABLE   **■SCHOLASTIC**
www.scholastic.co.uk

Assessment

Assessment grid

The following grid shows the main objectives and activities covered in this chapter. You can use the grid to locate activities that cover a particular focus that you are keen to monitor.

Objective	Page	Activity title
To use vocabulary relating to settlement, the environment and mapping.	82 83 84	How settlements developed The changing environment Mapping the way
To use vocabulary relating to the passage of time, aspects of society, and fact and opinion.	86 87 88	Language origins Family history autobiography Advice to time travellers
To use vocabulary relating to the four operations, shape and handling data.	90 91 92	Ballad of the builder Shapes in the news Explaining data handling
To use vocabulary relating to the explanation of scientific processes.	94 95 96	Wow – the car for me! Food survey Growing geraniums

Observation and record keeping

Look out for children using the vocabulary accurately across the curriculum and in their spoken as well as their written language. Where words have been used in texts that the children have read, or in written instructions such as in maths activities, note where children have a better understanding because they have learned the new vocabulary. This can be reflected in improved achievement against learning objectives and success criteria.

Assessment activity

- **What you need**
Photocopiable page 98 'Tropic Island'.
- **What to do**
Gather ideas for a brief piece of shared writing using your local area, covering historical and geographical aspects and including some of the vocabulary used in the chapter. Remind the class that they should do more than write a physical description of the island, they should write a sentence or two about its history. Ask them to highlight words that relate specifically to history. They can use some of the words more than once. Ask them to underline words to show when they have been used.

Differentiation

- Support children less sure of the vocabulary by guiding them through how to construct sentences using the words on the sheet. Alternatively, highlight several of the simpler words you would like them to try and use.

Further learning

- **Tropic Island:** Make a large-scale version of the map and display it together with written descriptions of aspects of the island, such as its climate, how things have changed due to building, natural disasters, the impact of technology, population growth and so on.
- **History:** During a historical theme remind the children of the vocabulary in the chapter and see how much of it they can incorporate into their spoken and written work. Encourage them to use selected words to guide their research, discussion or writing.
- **Science:** Assess how well the children understand technical vocabulary when they write about investigations they have completed.

Name:

Tropic island

■ Use as many of these words as you can to write about Tropic Island. Write about its history as well as describing what it is like.

route   ancient   beliefs   cause

agriculture   reason   population

approximately   weather

landscape   features   predict

discover   impact

recent   information   effect

suggest   explain

direction   problem

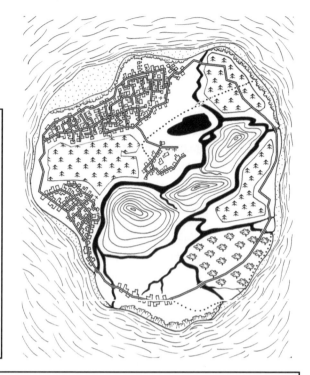

Word of the week

The Word of the week pages provide information on one word linked to each section in the chapter. Each word is described in some of the following categories: word definition, word origin, word family, alternative words, fascinating facts and activities. Not all categories are relevant to every word.

You can use the words as a focus to support your work on the different sections of the chapter. For example, you could create a display around it. The information is a starting point for a word focus. The words could form part of your classroom living word bank.

You could also use the word of the week as a springboard to inspire children to think about or research fascinating facts about words, find interesting quotations and to encourage them to use dictionaries and thesauruses.

Population

- **Word definition:** A noun meaning the number of people living in a place.
- **Word origin:** From Latin *populare* meaning to inhabit.
- **Word family:** Verb: *populate*.
- **Alternative words:** Community, people, dwellers, residents.
- **Fascinating facts:** The world's population hit 6.5 billion on 25 February 2006.
- **Activities:** Although associated mostly with geography, the word can also be used in an historical context, such as, *at that time there was a much smaller population*. Statistics for population growth can be studied in relation to a particular geographical location and linked with maps or social and economic change, thus linking geography and history.

> Linked section:
> Geography, page 81

Consequence

- **Word definition:** A noun meaning something that follows as a result.
- **Word origin:** From Latin *consequenti* meaning consequential.
- **Word family:** Adjective and noun: *consequent*.
- **Alternative words:** Effect, end, upshot, result.
- **Fascinating facts:** The game of consequences is an old parlour game. Each player takes a turn to write a sentence on a piece of paper then turn over the paper to hide what they have written and pass it to the next player. The categories are: a man's name, a woman's name, a place, he said to her, she said to him, the consequence, the outcome.
- **Activities:** Children can relate the word to result, which they may find initially easier to understand, for example, *one result of the Great Fire of London was that it got rid of the plague*, could be rephrased as, *one consequence of…*

> Linked section:
> History, page 85

Represent

- **Word definition:** A verb meaning to stand for or be a symbol; or to speak or act on behalf of others; or to claim to be.
- **Word origin:** From Latin *repraesentare* to bring about immediately.
- **Word family:** Noun: *representation*; adjective and noun: *representative*.
- **Alternative words:** stand for, substitute, imitate
- **Fascinating facts:** The study or interpretation of symbols is known as *symbology* and the study of signs is known as *semiotics*.
- **Activities:** Work with pictograms provides another opportunity to reinforce the concept, where symbols are chosen to represent the content of the pictogram. In other curriculum areas, badges, logos and flags can be used as symbols that represent different groups, clubs or countries, and children can design their own personal emblems that have pictures to represent important aspects of themselves.

Linked section: Mathematics, page 89

Process

- **Word definition:** A noun meaning a series of stages in producing goods or a series of events producing change. A verb meaning to perform a series of actions.
- **Word origin:** From French *proces* meaning journey.
- **Word family:** Noun: *procession*.
- **Alternative words:** Manner, operation, procedure, progress.
- **Fascinating facts:** The materials which we recycle have to go through a special process in order to be reused. You could research how this is done.

Linked section: Science, page 93

Fun with words

· ·

Here are some ideas to use for reinforcing the vocabulary in this chapter, focusing on its cross-curricular as well as subject-specific nature.

We're going on a word hunt
● Select a number of words from those studied and challenge the children to see how many different examples they can find of where and how the words are used, to demonstrate their cross-curricular nature. You could do this over a week, with the children recording their findings on a chart. At the end of the week, collect and compare results.

Subject glossaries
● Build up your own subject glossaries, with children's definitions of new words they encounter. These could include words related to maps, for example, how would they describe a swamp, a shingle beach or a cliff? What about an experiment, an effect or a prediction? Definitions could include illustrations, where appropriate.

A game of consequences
● Play 'Because' when studying past civilisations. Start a sentence by saying, for example, *Because the Roman army needed to get from place to place quickly…* and ask the children to complete it appropriately. So an answer might be …*they built straight roads and we still have some of them today*. They will be using the language of consequences or cause-and-effect to help their thinking and to reinforce prior learning. When the class is familiar with the game, encourage them to play it in groups, with a set of starter cards linked to your current historical focus. Each player selects one card from the set and has to complete the sentence, with the other players deciding whether it has been done correctly.

Themes
● Give groups of children a set of cards using words from any of the photocopiable sheets. Choose a theme that fits the words. Lay the cards out on the table. Each child must say a sentence about the theme that includes one of the words. As each word is used, remove it from the set.

What am I thinking?
● Share this game with the class before they play it themselves in pairs or groups. Make a laminated sheet, one for each chapter, showing the words covered in that chapter. Let the children choose a sheet and take turns to select one of the words for the others in their group to work out, by asking questions. Questions might be: *Is it a scientific word? Is it a noun/verb? Does it explain/describe something? Is it about shape? Would it be useful to a time traveller? Does it have to do with causes and effects?*

Chapter 5

Fun with words

Introduction

This chapter looks at words in the broadest sense, showing the children that forms of written communication are all around us, including the signs and symbols used in everyday life, which they may not even consider to be vocabulary, even though they can read and derive meaning from them. We also look at invented words, created by combining existing vocabulary, to serve a specific purpose, which is linked to the sections on word derivations found in Chapter 2. Finally, playing with nonsense words and how language looks on the page will give children a deeper understanding of the necessity for language conventions and rules.

In this chapter

Signs and symbols page 104	To combine words and images to communicate meaning.
Portmanteau words page 108	To use word knowledge to create new words.
Real words and nonsense words page 112	To investigate unusual uses of written language.
Word fun page 116	To make contextual use of language knowledge.
Assessment page 120	Activities and ideas to assess children's understanding of word structures and meanings.

Poster notes

Language all round (page 103)
This poster shows how writing is all around us. It can be used either as a stimulus to speaking and listening activities or for writing tasks. Here are some ideas:
● Have a general discussion with the children about environmental print. Ask them to spot the examples on the poster and give examples of their own.
● Ask the children to list all the different types of print communication they can see, such as, texting, posters, shop names, signs and menus.
● Look for examples of abbreviated language, such as on the mobile phone and the collection times on the post box.

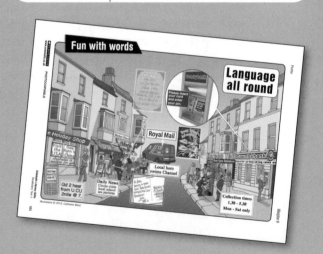

Illustrations © 2010, Catherine Ward.

Signs and symbols

Objective

To combine words and images to communicate meaning.

Background knowledge

Emoticons are emotional graphics, such as smiley faces and the myriad of cartoon-style images that are used in text messaging and emailing, to convey feelings and the tone of a message across the spectrum. *Onomatopoeia* describes words that imitate the sound associated with an action or an object, such as *plop*, *swish* or *crunch*.

Activities

This section focuses on elements of modern language usage that children come across every day. It harnesses the increasing use of emoticons, children's interest in comic-book texts and the language we all carry around on our clothing.

● **Photocopiable page 105 'Emoticons'**
This activity underlines the changing face of written language and the importance of visual communication, making it particularly useful for EAL learners and less confident readers, although it should be fun for everyone. Words and phrases for the smiley face should be written in the spaces on either side of the image. Encourage the children to think beyond just writing *happy* – remind them about synonyms.

● **Photocopiable page 106 'Zap! Boing! Boom!'**
Introduce the word *onomatopoeia* and explain its meaning. To make it easier for the children, break it down into syllables and practise saying it. Notice how many of the words describe some type of quick movement or loud noises. Note that the convention in comic books is for the writing to be in block capitals throughout, because the forms of capital letters are much less complex and less idiosyncratic than those of lowercase letters, making the text more dramatic.

● **Photocopiable page 107 'T-shirts'**
Children will be able to use their knowledge from the previous two activities to complete this activity. They should think of different wearers for each of the four T-shirts to avoid repetition of ideas and consider the language suited to their audience. Try using the well-known motif where a heart represents the word *love* to start them off.

Further ideas

● **Word wall:** Collect and display examples of onomatopoeia for all to enjoy. Ask the children to cut out or copy enlarged versions of favourite examples wherever they find them.

● **How are you today?:** Link the use of emoticons to PSHE, where children clip a clothes peg on to their choice of displayed emoticons, showing how they are feeling as they arrive at school. This develops children's self-awareness and consideration for others.

 What's on the CD-ROM

On the CD-ROM you will find:
● Printable versions of all three photocopiable pages.
● Interactive version of 'Zap! Boing! Boom!'.

Emoticons

■ How many different words and phrases can you think of that describe this symbol? Write your answers in the space around it.

■ In the shapes below, invent some of your own emoticons, and write words or phrases that could describe them. Think about what the shape could represent as well as the face.

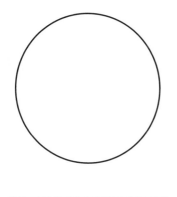  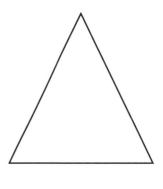

_____

_____

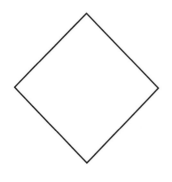 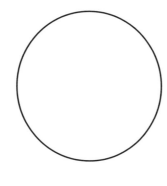 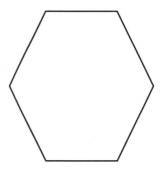

_____

_____

Name:

Zap! Boing! Boom!

■ Comic strips often use words that sound like their meaning, and illustrators have fun putting them in their drawings. Look at the illustrations below and write words that describe the sound they make.

_____ _____ _____ _____

_____ _____ _____ _____

_____ _____ _____ _____

_____ _____ _____ _____

PHOTOCOPIABLE   ■SCHOLASTIC
www.scholastic.co.uk

T-shirts

■ We often see T-shirts that have writing on them. Use emoticons or onomatopoeia to design some T-shirts that different types of people would enjoy wearing. Under each T-shirt, write who it is designed for.

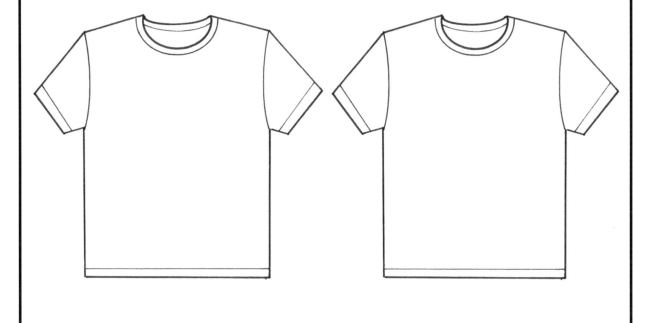

_____

_____

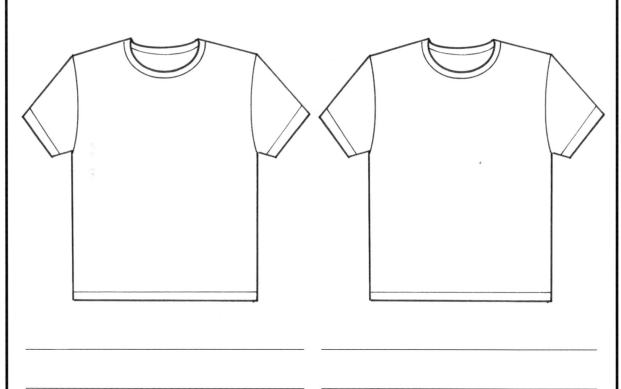

_____

_____

Illustrations © 2010, Catherine Ward.

Portmanteau words

Objective

To use word knowledge to create new words.

Background knowledge

Lewis Carroll is credited with inventing portmanteau words, when Humpty Dumpty explained them in *Alice Through the Looking Glass* as being *like a portmanteau* – there are two meanings packed into one, such as, *slithy* being a combination of *slimy* and *lithe*. Children may not know that a portmanteau is a type of suitcase and is itself a portmanteau word – a combination of *porter* (to carry) from the French, and *manteau* meaning mantle from Latin. These differ slightly from normal compound words, such as *windmill*, where two words are simply put side by side to create a new word. Although portmanteau words sound like nonsense, knowing their origins will add to children's vocabulary awareness. New additions to our language are often portmanteau words, used to describe new ideas or phenomena where two existing things are joined in a new way, such as *Bollywood*, which combines *Bombay* and *Hollywood*.

Activities

The children may not realise there are such things as portmanteau words, although there will be a number that they already know and use. This section makes them aware of these words and develops their understanding of how such new words come about.

- **Photocopiable page 109 'New words for old'**
Children will use their knowledge of existing words to create their own portmanteau words as described above. They should not limit themselves to just using the words on the sheet, but think of words related to the subject that they could blend together to form their new words. For example, *pasta sauce* could be *tomasta* – a combination of *tomato*, which is often used in pasta sauces, and *pasta*.
- **Photocopiable page 110 'Portmanteau rap'**
Having completed the previous activity, children have more freedom here to select words for any context. This works well as a paired activity. It would be good to hear some of the completed raps performed.
- **Photocopiable page 111 'Danger ahead'**
Encourage the children to think beyond the obvious portmanteau words in this activity. Let them compare their completed stories and ask them if it would make sense to someone who did not know the origins of the new words.

Further ideas

- **What's in the suitcase?:** As a portmanteau is a type of suitcase, display examples of these words inside suitcase shapes. The word is written on the lid, which is a flap that can be lifted to reveal, inside the suitcase, the two words that were combined to make it.
- **Advert:** Having created new words for products in the activity 'New words for old' children could go on to design a poster or television advert promoting their new product.

What's on the CD-ROM

On the CD-ROM you will find:
- Printable versions of all three photocopiable pages.
- Answers to 'New words for old'.

Portmanteau words

New words for old

■ Can you work out the two words that have been put together to make these new words? For example, **smog = smoke + fog**

Telethon = +	Motel = +
Jazzercise = +	Guesstimate = +

■ Imagine you are working for an advertising firm who have to invent new words for the latest products. Use this word-mixing idea to see what you can come up with. The first is done for you. (You may have to change the spelling a bit so your new word sounds right.)

Type of product	Using the words	New word
floor-cleaning liquid	floor + liquid	floriquid
toothpaste		
sports car		
cat food		
fizzy drink		
teddy		
sports magazine		
pasta sauce		
comfortable slippers		
comic book		

Name:

Portmanteau words

Portmanteau rap

■ Complete this rap by creating some portmanteau words of your own. You need to say which words you are mixing and then write the new word they make.

They're mixed-up words
So don't get confused
They're the coolest words you've ever used
So mix motor and hotel
And what've you got?
Motel! Yeah! That word is hot!

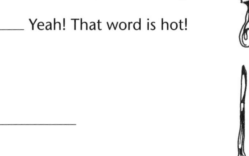

So turn on the tap

Of the portmanteau rap.

So mix _____

And what've you got?

_____ Yeah! That word is hot!

So turn on the tap

Of the portmanteau rap.

So mix _____

And what've you got?

_____ Yeah! That word is hot!

So turn on the tap

Of the portmanteau rap.

So mix _____

And what've you got?

_____ Yeah! That word is hot!

So turn on the tap

Of the portmanteau rap.

So mix _____

And what've you got?

_____ Yeah! That word is hot!

So turn on the tap

Of the portmanteau rap.

PHOTOCOPIABLE

■SCHOLASTIC
www.scholastic.co.uk

Illustrations © 2010, Catherine Ward.

Portmanteau words

Danger ahead

■ Invent your own portmanteau words to replace the words in bold in the story below.

Olaf and Gretchen crept carefully into the **dark forest**

_____. Ahead of them lay **great danger**

_____. At first they found it hard to see but gradually their

eyes got used to the **gloom** and **darkness** _____. They felt **scared**

and **nervous** _____ but were also **brave** and **determined**

_____ so they carried on. All around them they could

both **sense** and **hear** _____ **unknown creatures**

_____ who they felt sure were **tracking** and **following**

_____ them. Still they travelled on, **further** and **deeper**

_____ into the forest, not knowing what **surprises** and

shocks _____ lay ahead. Gretchen knew that Olaf would

save and **protect** _____

her from any difficulties, and Olaf knew

that Gretchen would not **scream** and **panic**

_____ if there were

dangers. They were, indeed, both full of **courage**

and **daring** _____.

Illustrations © 2010, Catherine Ward.

Real words and nonsense words

Objective

To investigate unusual uses of written language.

Background knowledge

Research published in 2003 (Kimura D, Seal B N. Psychol Rep. 2003 Aug; 93(1):263–4) found that while women have better recall of real words, this is not the case for nonsense words, so it would be interesting to see if this translates into your classroom. Decoding nonsense words is used as a component in the teaching of phonics, as an aid for children learning to read new words, and this can be a useful tool to use with less confident readers who are reluctant to use word-building skills. Playing with nonsense words can stimulate children's interest in and curiosity about words, which can carry over into the world outside the classroom and help them to develop an awareness of the changing nature of our language.

Activities

These activities bring the outside world into the classroom, drawing children's attention to yet another way in which our language (this time in written form) is constantly changing and how following the rules of how language works is important for understanding. When those rules are broken, communication becomes very difficult.

- **Photocopiable page 113 'Car number plates'**
Children may have their own examples of fun number plates. You will need to explain how the pronunciation of the individual letters is an intrinsic part of the way in which these words work, so that, for example, we can read the letters *B S U R* as *be as you are*.
- **Photocopiable page 114 'Shopping-list fun'**
This activity gives clues for the children to find smaller hidden words in longer words that they might encounter when they go shopping at the supermarket. Challenge early finishers to find more of their own examples.
- **Photocopiable page 115 'Jumbled instructions'**
The children will need to use their knowledge of letter patterns used in English to help them find where the spaces should be between the words. This can be done as a purely oral activity, working with a partner, or they could write the correct text in full on another sheet of paper.

Further ideas

- **Hidden words:** Build up a class word bank of any words the children have found where there are examples of smaller words hiding within longer words.
- **Mixed-up titles:** Children can rewrite book, television or film titles with the spaces in the wrong places between words for others to work out the correct title.

What's on the CD-ROM

On the CD-ROM you will find:
- Printable versions of all three photocopiable pages.
- Answers to all three photocopiable pages.
- Interactive versions of 'Car number plates' and 'Shopping-list fun'.

Name:

Real words and nonsense words

Car number plates

■ You can find hidden words and phrases on car number plates if you play around with the letters and numbers. Remember – you have to think about how you say the letters!

■ Numbers are sometimes used as letters, like this:

1 = L or I	2 = Z	3 = E	4 = A	5 = S
6 = B, G or C	7 = Y or T	8 = B	9 = G	0 = O

■ Write the real words and phrases for these number plates – some are easier than others. The first is done for you.

50 ICU	**4 KT**	**S4 SUE**
So I see you		

B16 DAY	**H34 VEN**	**F10 PSY**

D4 NDY	**WH 15 TLE**	**GH 05 TLY**

TOP 574R	**TEA 80Y**	**BAG 1T**

■ Now try making some of your own

Name:

Real words and nonsense words

Shopping-list fun

■ Words are hiding all around us. How many can you find? Start with the word:
supermarket

■ There are six smaller words hiding in there. Can you find all six?

■ What words are hiding in the shopping list below? Use the clues to help you.

Word	Clue	Hidden word
chocolate	It's not early!	
vegetables	Don't eat them on your knee.	
cereal	It's true, honest!	
drinks	You can skate here.	
delicatessen	My favourite pet.	
butcher	My fierce dog's name.	
pharmacy	It might hurt you.	
bread	You have to do this with the list!	
dairy	It's so light.	
salad	A young boy.	
flowers	Don't put them up high.	
rice	But it's cold!	
detergent	Stop the man. (Two words)	
kitchen	Scratch it then!	
tissues	It could be a problem.	
shampoo	A sandwich filling	
restaurant	Insects may relax here. (Two words)	

Jumbled instructions

■ When the company printed the instruction leaflet for how to fit together the bookcase Mrs Gray bought, they put the spaces between the words in the wrong places! What should the instructions say?

Beginb ychecking thaty ouhave allth eparts you need. You will fi ndalisto

f theminsid etheb ox. If anyp artsa remissing, call usonthe num berprovided an d w

ewill getthem to youa ssoo nas possible.

St epone: la you tall the par ts on theflo or so that youc an f in dthem easily.

S teptw o: put all t he pl as ticsh elfs upportsinto the ho leso nthe sid epieces

(A and B). Mak esu rethe y aretap pedin firmly.

Step th re e: scr e w th eside pie ceson to theb as e (C) withthelo ngests crews.

Stepfour: Fi xthet ops ection (D) on to t heside pieces.

St epfi ve: Fixtheb ack (E) onu sing thesm alln ails.

Step six: Fin all ysli det hesh elves intopo sit ion.

Word fun

To make contextual use of language knowledge.

Background knowledge

Providing children with activities designed to consolidate their learning in a fun and challenging way helps to embed new knowledge. Because much of the language used in this chapter is unusual, it challenges our concept of language, particularly in relation to what we should be teaching our children. However, it reflects not only how language changes, but also how it is used currently in the world beyond the classroom walls. Language is a tool that is used to convey ideas, emotions, facts and much more. To understand this through enjoyable means is empowering for children and helps to develop their communication skills.

Activities

This section provides the children with opportunities to use what they have learned about words in this chapter in games and challenges that include speaking and listening with a partner.

● **Photocopiable page 117 'Smoothies'**
Children will use their understanding of portmanteau words to play this game for two players. They may need to consider how their invented product name will be pronounced – the example provided can be read in more than one way.

● **Photocopiable page 118 'Theme park'**
Children can use what they know about signs and symbols to complete this activity. Remind them that there are things other than rides at theme parks – the images provided can refer to food, parking, litter and so on.

● **Photocopiable page 119 'Krazy Komix'**
Ask pairs of children to work on this activity together as an oral task or to write their ideas for possible images next to each of the words. Let the children select favourite images to draw, with the appropriate words next to them, which can then be displayed.

Further ideas

● **Smoothies:** Use design and technology to make cartons from nets of shapes. Invite the children to design the packaging, using their best ideas from the 'Smoothies' game on photocopiable page 117.

● **Theme-park map:** Using their ideas from photocopiable page 118 'Theme park', make a large map of a theme park on the wall, using the symbols and the children's ideas.

 ## What's on the CD-ROM

On the CD-ROM you will find:
● Printable versions of all three photocopiable pages.

Word fun

Smoothies

■ Play this game with a partner. The first player writes down two or three fruits or vegetables that will be blended together to make a new flavour of smoothie. The second player must invent a name to go on the packaging for the new flavour, using parts of the names of the ingredients. The first has been done for you.

■ Which would be your favourite flavour?

Ingredients	Name
apple, pear and orange	appearange

Name:

Theme park

■ A new brochure is being designed for a theme park. The pictures below have been chosen as symbols for different things in the park. Under each symbol, write what it might be used for. You may have more than one idea!

Word fun

Krazy Komix

■ On the Krazy Komix website, when you click on each of the words below, you hear a sound and see an image of what makes it. What might the images be? Draw your ideas on another piece of paper.

Assessment

Assessment grid

The following grid shows the main objectives and activities covered in this chapter. You can use the grid to locate activities that cover a particular focus that you are keen to monitor.

Objective	Page	Activity title
To combine words and images to communicate meaning.	105 106 107	Emoticons Zap! Boing! Boom! T-shirts
To use word knowledge to create new words.	109 110 111	New words for old Portmanteau rap Danger ahead
To investigate unusual uses of written language.	113 114 115	Car number plates Shopping-list fun Jumbled instructions
To make contextual use of language knowledge.	117 118 119	Smoothies Theme park Krazy Komix

Observation and record keeping

Note those children who show particular understanding or creativity, particularly in paired or group activities. Note also the children who seem confused by new or nonsense words. If their everyday vocabulary is poor, this may be a step too far for them, so they may need extra support. Using visual clues may help. Encourage children to keep their own list of new words – this can help to assess their growing vocabulary. Look out for children making use of the new words in both speech and writing.

Assessment activity

● **What you need**

Photocopiable page 121 'Book sort', piece of plain paper for every child, scissors, glue sticks.

● **What to do**

Remind the class of the types of words covered in this chapter: portmanteau, onomatopoeia and nonsense words, along with signs and symbols. Ask the children to cut, sort and paste the book titles into categories that they select. Explain that some of the titles have actual words that are easy clues, but others will need a little more thought (e.g. 'Registration Marks of Britain and Ireland' refers to car registrations – symbols that identify cars individually).

Differentiation

● Less confident readers may need the titles read for them or discussion with an adult to decide how to categorise the titles. Referring back to the activities they have done should help this.

● Challenge more confident readers to add titles of their own to those provided.

Further learning

● **What's inside?:** Let the children choose one of the titles from the assessment activity to write a blurb that might be on the back of the book.

● **Comics:** Look closely at the language used in comics. Ask the children why they think the noise and action words are displayed prominently in shapes. Invite the children to rewrite these scenes as a narrative.

● **Signs and symbols:** Provide the children with symbols from the environment, such as road signs or religious symbols. Discuss what the symbols represent and why we sometimes use symbols rather than words.

Assessment

Book sort

■ Mrs Patel, the librarian, has just received a delivery of new books for her library. Help her to decide where they should go.

■ Cut out the titles, sort them into categories that you think go together, then paste them on to a sheet of paper, labelling your categories to explain how you have grouped them.

Registration marks of Britain and Ireland	**And frogs go 'plop'!**
Logos on your computer	**Camcorder guide**
The best motels in the world	**1T5 MAG1C**
Professor Blob on the planet Zargon	**Road signs**
Collywobbles and nincompoops	**Amy and the kangaphant**
Popular T-shirt designs	**Collecting fanzines**
Smiley faces for your emails	**Scrunch!**
Zap! Crash! Boing! All about Superman	**Soap powder names of the 20th century**
The sweesh of the curtain	**My friend the werevamp**

Word of the week

The Word of the week pages provide information on one word linked to each section in the chapter. Each word is described in some of the following categories: word definition, word origin, word family, alternative words, fascinating facts and activities. Not all categories are relevant to every word.

You can use the words as a focus to support your work on the different sections of the chapter. For example, you could create a display around it. The information is a starting point for a word focus. The words could form part of your classroom living word bank.

You could also use the word of the week as a springboard to inspire children to think about or research fascinating facts about words, find interesting quotations and to encourage them to use dictionaries and thesauruses.

Symbol

- **Word definition:** A noun meaning a mark or a sign with a special meaning.
- **Word origin:** From Latin *symbolum* meaning token or mark.
- **Word family:** Adjective: *symbolic*; noun: *symbolism.*
- **Alternative words:** Logo, motif, representation, emblem.
- **Fascinating facts:** The aster flower is a symbol of love and mistletoe is a symbol of peace and joy.
- **Activities:** In ICT, icons in commonly used program can be collected in a class ICT glossary, recognising them as symbols for the actions they represent. Looking at religious artefacts can help children to understand that not only words and images are symbols, but elements of religious practice are symbolic of important events or concepts.

> Linked section:
> Signs and symbols,
> page 104

Blend

- **Word definition:** A verb meaning to mix and a noun meaning an act or manner of blending, or a sequence of two or more consonants.
- **Word origin:** From Middle English *blenden* meaning to mix.
- **Word family:** Noun: *blender.*
- **Alternative words:** Mix, fusion, compound.
- **Fascinating facts:** The largest gazpacho soup (4520 litres) was made on 2 August 2008 they used industrial-sized hand blenders to blend the tomatoes, cucumber, peppers, onion and garlic.
- **Activities:** Use the word simply when colour-mixing paint in art lessons, as a tangible way for children to understand its meaning.

Talk about blending sounds together to form words and parts of words. This is particularly useful when children are decoding unknown words, and using its opposite, segmenting, when learning spellings.

> Linked section:
> Portmanteau words,
> page 108

Novel

- **Word definition:** An adjective meaning something new and different to anything else. And a noun meaning a story of length.
- **Word origin:** Adjective: from Latin *novellus* meaning fresh and young. Noun: from Italian *novella* meaning a new kind of story.
- **Word family:** Noun: *novelist, novelty*.
- **Alternative words:** Adjective: contemporary, different, fresh, innovative. Noun: fiction, narrative, story, tale.
- **Fascinating facts:** The printing press was first developed in Germany by Johann Gutenburg in around 1439. This helped to bring literature to the masses.
- **Activities:** They may not be aware of the word as a noun, as children at this age usually refer to longer reads as 'chapter books', but once they know these texts as 'novels' they can be asked to work out why they are so named, in relation to the meaning of the word as a verb. Link the idea of novelty to ideas and inventions of the past, such as Edison and the light bulb, the first umbrella and so on.

Linked section: Real words and nonsense words, page 112

Observant

- **Word definition:** An adjective meaning to pay close attention.
- **Word origin:** Derives from Latin *observare* meaning to watch.
- **Word family:** Verb: *observe*; noun: *observatory, observation*.
- **Alternative words:** Attentive, perceptive, watchful.
- **Fascinating facts:** The girl's name *Gregoriana* is Greek meaning observant.
- **Activities:** To foster the habit of being observant and noticing things that others might miss, let the children enjoy the illustrations in the many picture books by Anthony Browne, who specialises in imaginative and bizarre additions and alterations in his images. Try *Piggybook* (Dragonfly Books) where parts of everyday objects in one family's house gradually begin to look like pigs' faces, or *Changes* (Walker Books) where some strange things happen.

Linked section: Word fun, page 116

Fun with words

· ·

Here are some further ideas, including quick starter activities, games and longer projects to reinforce the learning in this chapter.

Feelings
● Children draw an emoticon on a whiteboard. Others guess what it represents. See how many different suggestions they can come up with.

Wearing words
● Have a 'Read me' day when children wear clothes that have writing on them and encourage everyone to read everyone else. Extend this to involve the whole school, perhaps as part of World Book Day, or as a fundraising event.

Sharing comics
● Ask the children to bring in comics they have read to make a class box that can be shared. Good examples of onomatopoeia can be added to a class collection.

Number-plate game
● Challenge the children to think of words that include letters in car number plates, in the order in which they occur. For example, from 'AL 58 WTN' you can make 'ALWays' or 'WaiTiNg'. As an alternative game, find phrases or sentences using the letters to start each word, such as *Ants Leap While They Nod* (nonsense is acceptable).

Word match
● Play a game where four or five words are displayed and the children have to see how many portmanteau words they can invent by combining any of the given words. Challenge them to also provide definitions for their new words.

Crossed words
● The clues on photocopiable page 114 'Shopping-list fun' are similar to those in crosswords, so provide a range of crosswords for the children to complete at registration time or even a wet playtime.

Find me!
● Challenge the class to find words that have smaller words hidden in them, for partners to discover. This could be a quick five- or ten-minute dictionary activity.

Emoticon faces
● Encourage one child to make facial expressions for others to guess the emotion they are trying to convey.

Guess my word
● Ask individual children or pairs to invent a portmanteau word. The others should work out what the two original words were and guess what the newly-created word could mean. The class could be given a particular genre for their new words, such as fantasy, horror or adventure.

All mixed up
● Extend photocopiable page 115 'Jumbled instructions' by asking the children to write two or three sentences on a whiteboard, giving instructions for carrying out a simple task, where they have deliberately put the spaces in the wrong place. They then challenge each other to read the jumbled text correctly. This could also be done on the computer.

Word bank

This word bank provides differentiated examples of further vocabulary related to each of the chapters in the book. These lists can be used alongside the posters that also support each chapter. While some of the suggested words can be linked to specific sections of a chapter, for example 'Synonyms for nice' in Chapter 1 relates to the third section of that chapter; other lists are more generic and could apply to a variety of activities. The word bank for Chapter 2, for instance, incorporates words from different languages as well as focusing on prefixes and suffixes in their own right, while Chapter 4's cross-curricular words are deliberately not confined to any particular subject, as they can be used in many contexts. The inclusion of 'Adverbs for time' is to help children to be aware of adverbs other than those ending in '-ly', thus broadening their understanding of how adverbs work. Likewise, it is useful for children to have a working vocabulary with which to discuss language itself, so a section on meta-language has been included.

The word banks can be used to support activities in the Fun with words sections of each chapter and also to support additional activities alongside those in the book. For example, use the 'Synonyms for nice' for a piece of descriptive writing and use the 'Prefixes' and 'Suffixes' to search for definitions in a dictionary. Use the 'Verbs describing movement' as a basis for drama, and display 'Adverbs of time' and 'cross-curricular words' for general use in writing activities. Introduce the 'Meta-language – words about language' when appropriate over the course of the year, and use the 'Environmental word' lists for potential outcomes.

Adjectives for impact

Chapter 1

Basic	Intermediate	Advanced
tasty	delicious	scrumptious
worried	anxious	concerned
crafty	cunning	shrewd
scared	terrified	alarmed
crunchy	crackling	rustling
bright	dazzling	vivid

Synonyms for nice

Basic	Intermediate	Advanced
excellent	superb	exceptional
great	pleasant	amiable
kind	polite	considerate
lovely	attractive	delightful
beautiful	charming	kindly
friendly	gentle	admirable

Prefixes Chapter 2

Basic	Intermediate	Advanced
microscope	microfilm	microcosm
microchip	microlight	microbe
automatic	autobiography	automaton
telescope	telephoto	telecommunication
teletext	telegram	telephonist
geography	geology	geometry

Suffixes

Basic	Intermediate	Advanced
action	friction	communication
fraction	exhibition	inclination
mobile	incredible	digestible
possible	responsible	illegible
valuable	desirable	dependable
miserable	sociable	irritable

Verbs describing movement Chapter 3

Basic	Intermediate	Advanced
dash	scramble	hobble
scamper	shuffle	stalk
creep	wander	stagger
stride	plod	prance
glide	waddle	strut
tip-toe	sneak	amble

Adverbs of time

Basic	Intermediate	Advanced
now	instantly	immediately
next	forever	presently
before	recently	formerly
yet	afterwards	while
since	nowadays	continually
until	already	occasionally

Cross-curricular words   Chapter 4

Basic		Intermediate		Advanced	
explain	match	investigate	compare	suggest	comparison
reason	same	experiment	similar	consequence	observe
problem	different	describe	discover	solution	deduce
solve	prove	estimate	evidence	systematic	demonstrate
decide	choose	predict	discuss	classify	conclude
information	record	data	select	interpret	evaluate

Meta-language – Words about language   Chapter 5

Basic	Intermediate	Advanced
rhyming	alliteration	onomatopoeia
library	symbol	assonance
blurb	portmanteau	appropriate
fiction	definition	graphic
poet	genre	categories
rhythm	abbreviation	novel

Environmental words

Basic	Intermediate	Advanced
sign	emoticon	digital
poster	logo	jingle
text	flyer	design
leaflet	junk mail	innovative
email	advertisement	packaging
menu	persuasive	brochure

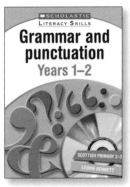
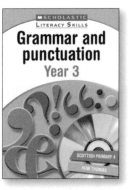
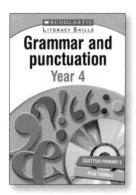
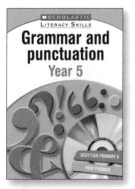
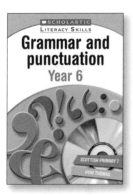
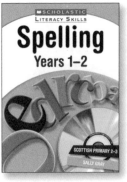
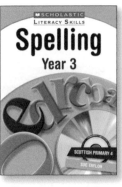
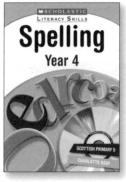
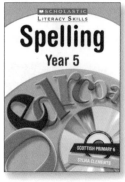

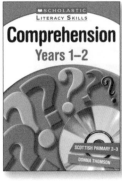
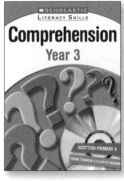
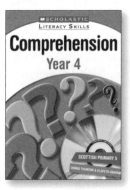
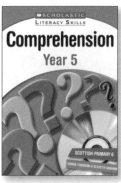
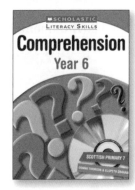